Standing
for
Something

D0012879

Standing
for
Something

10 NEGLECTED VIRTUES
THAT WILL HEAL OUR
HEARTS AND HOMES

GORDON B. HINCKLEY

Foreword by Mike Wallace

THREE RIVERS PRESS
NEW YORK

Published by Three Rivers Press, New York, New York.
Member of the Crown Publishing Group.

Random House, Inc. New York, Toronto, London, Sydney, Auckland
www.randomhouse.com

THREE RIVERS PRESS is a registered trademark and the Three Rivers Press colophon is a trademark of Random House, Inc.

Originally published in hardcover by Times Books in 2000.

Printed in the United States of America

Library of Congress Cataloging-in-Publication Data

Hinckley, Gordon Bitner, 1910–
    Standing for something : 10 neglected virtues that will heal our hearts and homes / Gordon B. Hinckley; with a foreword by Mike Wallace.
    Includes bibliographical references.
    1. Christian life—Mormon authors.   2. Virtues.   I. Title
BX8656.H57 2000
241'.4—dc21

                                                          99-048596

ISBN 0-609-80725-0

10 9

Contents

PART TWO
The Guardians of Virtue

Foreword

F our years ago, I was taken aback by an unexpected invitation to a luncheon at the Harvard Club in New York City. From prior experience, I figured the food would be mediocre at best, but since I'd been asked to break bread with the hitherto mysterious octogenarian president of the Mormon Church, and because the invitation was tendered on the president's behalf by a Jewish-owned public relations firm, it was too tantalizing to pass up.

I'd been trying for decades to get some top Mormon leader, *any* top Mormon leader, to talk to 60 MINUTES about himself and his church, and I'd regularly been turned down. Mormon friends of mine had volunteered to put in a good word; they'd let the Salt Lake City hierarchy understand that an investigation was not what I had in mind, but rather an exploration of what kind of individual led the Mormons, how did he get his job, what about Mormons and polygamy, what about Mormons and black folks, and did the leaders of the Mormon Church really believe that tale about Joseph Smith finding himself anointed at the age of fourteen on a farm in upstate New York? Merely the kind of nosy questions we regularly put to all manner of highly placed figures on 60 MINUTES. We hardly expected "Yes" for an answer, any more than we expected "Yes" for an answer to our similar invitations to the pope of the Roman Catholic Church.

So I was totally unprepared for a cordial, even a sunny greeting from Gordon B. Hinckley at the luncheon. And I was still hesitant when, following his postprandial remarks, he threw the floor open for questions from any and all of us. Timorously, I wondered aloud to him whether he might entertain the notion of an interview-cum-profile for 60 MINUTES. President Hinckley's bespectacled eyes literally twinkled as he good-naturedly allowed that it sounded like an appealing notion; after all, he really had nothing to hide, and he imagined he'd have little difficulty handling whatever queries I loosed at him. He'd heard and answered worse, he was sure, during his young missionary years in London, where he'd taken on whatever the skeptics and nonbelievers had thrown at him in his Hyde Park appearances and/or confrontations.

So all the necessary details and arrangements were quickly made. He put at our disposal just about anyone we wanted to talk with from the Salt Lake infrastructure, he put up no objections to our talking to his critics inside and outside the church, he gave us all the camera time we needed, and when we asked for a second sit-down some weeks after the first, so that we could put some questions we'd missed in the first go-around, he was perfectly agreeable. It turned out he was as good as his promised word back at the Harvard Club.

As a result, we came away with a fascinating profile of a genuinely remarkable man. Which confounded more than a few Mormon friends of mine who let me know, later, how chary they'd been when they first learned what I'd been up to. Their original take: Hinckley's going to talk to Wallace? Is he dotty? Doesn't he understand what can happen when 60 MINUTES sets out to do one of its hatchet jobs?

Well, what happened was that my 60 MINUTES colleagues and I learned, from the time we spent with Gordon Hinckley and his wife, from his staff, and from other Mormons who talked to us, that this warm and thoughtful and decent and optimistic leader of the Mormon Church fully deserves the almost universal admiration that he gets. I know that may sound more than a trifle corny coming from a dyed-in-the-wool, jaded, New York-based reportorial cynic. But it was difficult not to arrive at that conclusion after talking not only *with* him, but *about* him with hardheaded folks such as Orrin Hatch and Bill Marriott and Steve Young and Dave Checketts. The last-named individual runs Madison Square Garden in New York and was one of the Mormons who had worried about what could result if President Hinckley laid himself open to our abrasions. Checketts was so surprised when he saw our piece on the air that he told me (I mention this only in the interest of full disclosure) to call him any time I had trouble getting tickets to a fight or a basketball game at the Garden.

Further in the interest of full disclosure, as an 81-year-old myself, perhaps I can be excused for recalling the exchange I had with President Hinckley near the end of that 60 MINUTES profile.

Wallace: There are those who say: "This is a gerontocracy . . . this is a church run by old men."

Hinckley: Isn't it wonderful to have a man of maturity at the head? A man who isn't blown about by every wind of doctrine?

Wallace: Absolutely, as long as he's not dotty.

Hinckley: Thank you for the compliment.

He is far from dotty. As you read on, you'll find an agile, thoughtful, and engaging mind bent on persuading us to ruminate, along with him, on old-fashioned values: by name, Virtue and Integrity.

MIKE WALLACE

Introduction

The Secularization of America

If we are to continue to have the freedoms that came of the inspiration of the Almighty to our Founding Fathers, we must return to the God who is their true Author.

I am a churchman. I readily acknowledge, therefore, that my perspective is a reflection of my upbringing, my training, the virtues and principles in which I believe, and my personal observations as I near age ninety.

The twentieth century was just a decade old when I was born to loving, God-fearing parents. In 1910, a male born in the United States could expect to live to age fifty, and I am happy to say that I have bettered that expectation considerably.

In fact, I still feel young, with a love for life and its challenges and pleasures. My life has been rich because it has been filled with problems to solve and associations to savor. I have wrestled with dilemmas large and small. I have known something of discouragement and, on a few occasions, have felt the exhilaration of achievement. I feel a great sense of gratitude for the marvelous and generous blessings of the Almighty.

As a result of good health, long life, and various opportunities and obligations arising from responsibilities in The

Church of Jesus Christ of Latter-day Saints, which I have the privilege of representing, I have tromped and traveled around this world for the better part of ninety years. I have visited more than 150 countries, many of them dozens of times. I have walked on China's Great Wall, toured Vietnam during its season of intense conflict and seen firsthand the spoils and ravages of war, listened to bullets zing by my hotel window during a coup in Seoul, mourned with the survivors of a deadly shipwreck in the South Pacific, searched for earthquake victims in Peru, and viewed hurricane devastation in Honduras and Nicaragua.

Such experiences have taken me across the seas south and west and east. The world's sights have been glorious to behold. I have wondered at the symmetry of Fujiyama in Japan and marveled at the transcendent beauty of the great mountains of Switzerland, France, and Italy. I have seen the Taj Mahal by moonlight in Agra, India; the orchards of Russia in the bloom of spring; and the rice lands of China at harvest time. I have admired the pampas of Argentina and the towering peaks of Bolivia, and walked in the great and beautiful cities of Europe. I have known the beauties of New Zealand, the expanse of Australia, the highlands of the Andes, the exotic fauna of the Amazon, and the peaks and plains of every nation in South America.

I love the peoples of the world! I love the sights and smells, the grand varieties of culture with their costumes, customs, and music; eyes dark and light, hair black and blonde, and the incredible range of creativity in everything from architecture to food. I believe this world to be the creation of Jehovah, and I delight at its diversity.

But as much as I love the peoples and places of the world, I return from each trip abroad with a peculiar love for my homeland. Many times, as I've flown over the Atlantic or Pacific en route home, the words of Henry Van Dyke have come into my mind:

'Tis fine to see the Old World, and travel up and down
Among the famous palaces and cities of renown,
To admire the crumbly castles and the statues of the kings,—
But now I think I've had enough of antiquated things.
So it's home again, and home again, America for me!
My heart is turning home again, and there I long to be,
In the land of youth and freedom beyond the ocean bars,
Where the air is full of sunlight and the flag is full of stars.

I love America!

I love America for its great and brawny strength, the products of its vital factories, and the science of its laboratories. I love it for the great intellectual capacity of its people, for their generous hearts and helping hands. I love America's tremendous spiritual heritage and strengths. It is unique among the nations of the earth—in its discovery, in its birth as a nation, in the amalgamation of the races and cultures that have come to its shores, in the consistency and strength of its government.

I love America for the tremendous genius of its scientists, its researchers, its laboratories, its universities, and the tens of thousands of facilities devoted to the increase of human health and comfort, to the sustenance of life, to improved communication and transportation. Its great throbbing and thriving industries have blessed the entire world. The standard of living of its people has been the envy of the entire earth. Its farmlands have yielded an abundance undreamed of in most lands of the world. The entrepreneurial environment that has sustained its industry has been the envy of and model for all nations.

My wife and I first visited Jerusalem long ago, before the 1967 war. It was then a divided city. We retained the services of a guide who was an Arab, and, during our tour, we stood on an elevation where we could see the other side of Jerusalem. With tears in his eyes, this man pointed to the home from which he had been dispossessed. And then he said with deep emotion, "You belong to the greatest nation on the face of the earth. Yours is the only nation that has been victorious in war and never claimed any territory as a prize of conquest. Your people have given millions, even billions, to the poor of the earth and never asked for anything in return. Rather, even after coming off as conqueror, you have poured yet other billions to revive those who had been your enemies in bloody conflict."

I had never thought of this significant perspective before. In no instance during my lifetime—not in the First World War or the Second, not in the Korean War or Vietnam or the Persian Gulf—did our nation seize and hold territory for itself as a prize of conquest. To the contrary: On a train from Fukuoka, on the south island of Japan, to Tokyo, I have passed mile upon mile of great, modern steel mills built largely with money from the United States following the devastation of Japan. Now the Japanese are our tremendous competitors in the markets of the world. Not only did we *not* seize territory at the end of World War II, but we provided the impetus that has led to their superiority in many business enterprises. Surely there is no story like this in all of recorded history!

On another occasion, I accompanied the U.S. Agricultural Attaché to the docks of Bombay, in India, and there counted fourteen freighters in the harbor, each waiting to unload its cargo of wheat. We stood there for an hour as ton after ton of wheat from the fields of America was lifted out of the hulls of those ships. That grain spelled life to millions of the hungry of that land. When we returned to the attaché's office, he gathered his tabulations from his files and sat down to enter them into a calculating machine. Later, he concluded that the delivery of American wheat to India that year amounted to all of the grain grown in the United States from Colorado westward. Ours is a generous country that has been quick to respond when others are in need.

I especially love America for its great spiritual strength. It is a land of churches and synagogues, of temples and tabernacles, of pulpits and altars. We have on our coinage and our currency a national motto. It simply says, "In God We Trust." I believe that this is the foundation on which this nation was established: an unequivocal trust in the power of the Almighty to guide and defend us.

The hand of the Almighty was manifest on this continent even before the United States of America came into being. I have walked aboard the re-creation of the *Mayflower*, that tiny craft in which a hundred men, women, and children crossed the Atlantic in search of freedom to worship God according to the dictates of their conscience. Before even disembarking from the *Mayflower* and stepping ashore after their long and grueling voyage, our Pilgrim fathers drafted and signed the Compact that became the instrument of their governance, the first such document drafted on this continent. It began with these words:

"In the name of God, amen." It went on to say that the signers "by these presents solemnly and mutually in the presence of God, and one another, covenant and combine ourselves together into a civil body politic ... and by virtue hereto do enact ... such just and equal laws ... as shall be thought most meet and convenient for the general good of the colony." This was the first charter of civil liberty drawn in America, the first of a succession of instruments that became the foundation of the miracle that is America.

Consider George Washington, Benjamin Franklin, James Madison, Patrick Henry, Thomas Jefferson, and their associates who signed the Declaration of Independence or participated in the Constitutional Convention. It is my conviction that although we have had a few great leaders since then, there has not been before or since so large a group of talented, able, dedicated, and inherently good men as those whom we call the Founding Fathers of our nation. For as long as they lived and led, they acknowledged the hand of the Almighty in the affairs of this republic.

Envision the scene at the Continental Congress assembled in Philadelphia in the muggy June of 1776. There was drafted a Declaration of Independence, which concluded, "And for the support of this Declaration, with a firm reliance on the protection of Divine Providence, we mutually pledge to each other our Lives, our Fortunes and our sacred Honor." Those who signed that document gave their lives; some of them literally rotted away as prisoners of war. They gave their fortunes. But they kept their sacred honor.

The war for independence followed. That was a time of crisis in our history, not alone because all the power of Britain was against the Colonies but more so because jealousy, bickering, and recrimination among the colonists resulted in a lack of adequate support for the army. That army, at its peak, numbered only 35,000 men. As acknowledged by some of those who were there, the God of Heaven fought its battles.

When the war ended, the bickering continued. But our Founding Fathers were men whom the God of Heaven had raised up, men who saw with a greater vision and dreamed a better and more inspired dream, men more concerned with the good of the whole than with their own personal comfort, reputations, or image before the people. On May 14, 1787, fifty-five of them met in Philadelphia. The heat of that summer was oppressive, the worst in the memory of the city's residents. There were differences of opinion, sharp and deep and bitter. But somehow, under the inspiration of the Almighty, there was forged the Constitution of the United States. On September 17, 1787, thirty-nine of the fifty-five attendees signed the document. It began with this remarkable preamble:

> We, the People of the United States, in order to form a more perfect Union, establish Justice, insure domestic Tranquillity, provide for the common Defence, promote the general Welfare, and secure the Blessings of Liberty to ourselves and our posterity, do ordain and establish this Constitution for the United States of America.

Of it, the great William Gladstone said later: "As the British Constitution is the most subtle organism which has proceeded from . . . progressive history, so the American Constitution is, so far as I can see, the most wonderful work ever struck off at a given time by the brain and purpose of man."

The Constitution and Bill of Rights form the keystone of our nation.

It is my conviction that they came not alone of the brain and purpose of humans, but of the inspiration of the Almighty—that God Himself directed the founding of this nation. The document wrought by the men of 1787 in the miracle of Philadelphia provided for orderly changes of government, and the wonder of it is that, through two centuries, order has been preserved and observed.

Today, we stand on the shoulders of those who preceded us, men and women of courage and conviction who, in the midst of adversity, put their trust in the Almighty and worked endlessly to make their dreams come true; men and women who had nothing to sustain them but hope and faith, but who nonetheless brought to pass the nation that now graces this land.

I am not one to believe that all was good in the long ago and that all is bad today. For many reasons, I proclaim that *this* is the greatest age the world has known. But there is trouble in the land.

Today, we face challenges the Founding Fathers could not have possibly imagined or conceived; our societal challenges would have horrified them. We have come through wars, both civil and international, with victory, and have found peace. Yet now we are a people of contention. Strident and accusatory voices are heard in argument across the nation. We rose from scratch to become the greatest industrial power in the history of the earth, but we have lost some of our competitive edge, and have seen other nations move ahead of us in various fields, in both research and production. We spend billions of our resources in litigation one against another. Our spiritual power is sapped by a floodtide of pornography, by a debilitating epidemic of the use of narcotics and drugs that destroy both body and mind, and by a declining moral standard that is alarming and devastating to relationships, families, and the integrity of our nation as a whole.

We are forgetting God, whose commandments we have neglected and in some cases forgotten, and which we seem reluctant—or too undisciplined—to obey. In too many ways, we have substituted human sophistry for the wisdom of the Almighty.

America is still strong, but destructive forces have been and are at work. There is a serious unsteadiness in our country's stance in terms of morality, ethics, principles, and behavior. We as a people and a nation have increasingly neglected and abandoned time-honored virtues that have been proven through the centuries to keep human beings individually, and therefore collectively, strong.

These problems are only symptomatic of many other problems we have as a people. During recent years, polls and circumstances have suggested that an unprecedented majority of Americans believe that the private lives of public officials need not be considered as a factor in their eligibility for public office, and that private morality has no connection with public behavior and credibility. I am more deeply concerned about the growing moral deficit than I am about the monetary deficit.

For a good while, there has been going on in this nation a process that I have termed the secularization of America. The single most substantial factor in the degeneration of the values and morals of our society is that we as a nation are forsaking the Almighty, and I fear that He will begin to forsake us. We are shutting the door against the God whose sons and daughters we are.

I have heard Margaret Thatcher, former Prime Minister of Great Britain, say on more than one occasion, "You use the name of Deity in the Declaration of Independence and in the Constitution of the United States, and yet you cannot use it in the schoolroom." Her words are a rebuke and an indictment of America. Reverence for the Almighty, gratitude for His beneficent blessings, pleadings for His guidance, and a willingness to acknowledge His omniscience and omnipotence are increasingly being dropped from our public discourse.

Oaths of office and sworn promises to tell the truth in other legal procedures have traditionally concluded with the phrase, "So help me God." Several years ago, the state of New Jersey passed a law banishing the mention of God from state courtroom oaths. Following this action by the New Jersey legislature, a county judge decided to ban Bibles for such oaths "because you-know-Who is mentioned inside." And in recent years, the Boy Scouts of America have been attacked because of the language in the Scout Oath: "On my honor, I will do my best to do my duty to God and my country."

Contrast such attitudes with that of George Washington, expressed more than two hundred years ago in his First Inaugural Address:

> It would be peculiarly improper to omit, in this first offi-
> cial act, my fervent supplications to that Almighty Being,
> who rules over the universe, who presides in the councils

of nations, and whose providential aids can supply every human defect, that His benediction may consecrate to the liberties and happiness of the people of the United States a government instituted by themselves for these essential purposes.

People who carry in their hearts a strong conviction concerning the living reality of the Almighty and their accountability to Him for what they do with their lives are far less likely to become enmeshed in problems that inevitably weaken society. The loss of this conviction, the almost total secularizing of our public attitudes, has been largely responsible for the terrible social illnesses now running rampant among us.

In short, we are turning our hearts away from the God of the universe. *Divine law* has become a meaningless phrase. What was once so commonly spoken of as sin is now referred to as nothing more than poor judgment. Blatant dishonesty is openly referred to and excused as "misleading others." Virtue is too often neglected, if not scorned or ridiculed as old-fashioned, confining, unenlightened. What was once considered transgression has now been labeled merely *misbehavior*, which we have come to not only tolerate but, in too many cases, rationalize, accept, and even embrace.

In earlier days, children and families were regarded as gifts from God, and a great majority of parents both acknowledged and accepted their responsibility to nurture their children and bring them up in understanding, light, and truth. Work was a virtue to be enthroned as the enhancement of human dignity.

Marriage was once generally regarded as a sacred sacrament, but, for the populace as a whole, it is becoming an increasingly secular ceremony. Now, the epidemic of divorce rages on as an alarming number of adults choose to set aside the binding contracts they have made rather than subject themselves to the effort, the struggle of righting wrongs and repairing relationships. While parents quarrel, children suffer. The very foundation of their lives—a secure and happy home—is pulled from under them. We are losing something that speaks of accountability, not only to one another but to God who is our Father and who will stand in judgment upon us.

We need to be acutely aware of and concerned about our children, speaking of them as a whole. I worry about the millions who come into the world with handicaps, seemingly impossible to overcome—children whose lives are blighted by neglect and abuse, children who have limitless capacity but almost no opportunity. In the long term, this may well be the most serious problem facing our nation because its consequences multiply and reach forward through generations.

Lack of self-discipline and of a sense of responsibility is one of the fruits of the increasing secularization of our society. I was appalled to read not long ago that, in one community, a proposal was made that young women be paid a dollar a day for not becoming pregnant. How pathetic! Where is our sense of values?

Between 1972 and 1990, there were twenty-seven million abortion procedures performed in the United States. Think of it. What is happening to our concept of the sanctity of life?

The terrible blight of gangs affects our cities and our youth. These young men and women—many of whom are enticed into gangs in an attempt to imitate the feelings of belonging that should be supplied in the home—scheme, roam, destroy

property, and fight. They murder one another as well as innocent victims who happen to get in their way. They are an ill-
begotten lot of young people who drift in a mire of terror and
whose lives—if they survive—lead only to incarceration.

We try to gamble our way into prosperity, and, in the process, we further impoverish ourselves. In 1994 alone, Americans spent 482 billion dollars on gambling—more than they
spent that year on movies, sports, music, cruise ships, and
theme parks combined. Not long ago, lotteries were forbidden
by law. Now, in many of our states, they are commonly viewed
as a painless and politically expedient way to tax people without really taxing them, and to help balance budgets that are
often out of line because of the unrestrained, undisciplined
spending of public officials who have squandered their constituents' resources.

Too many of our youth, at alarmingly young ages, have access to and use drugs. And we see account after horrifying account of school massacres—children killing children, parents,
and teachers.

We have in this nation more than a million people in
prison, and we cannot build facilities fast enough to accommodate the accelerating need.

Can there be any doubt that a great sickness has invaded
our land, and that healing is desperately needed in our hearts
and in our homes? Our value system is deteriorating and
crumbling before our eyes. Secular self-sufficiency has replaced worship in the lives of many.

That is the bad news. As we enumerate all our ills, the situation may appear hopeless. But there is great reason to have hope,
for there is a remedy. Our sickness is not difficult to diagnose,

nor is the remedy complicated to prescribe. Healing in our hearts and in our homes, and subsequently throughout society, will begin to occur when we individually and collectively return to the code of ethics and the canons of divine truth that our honored forefathers lived by.

We can treat and even cure the sickness that afflicts us by reenthroning the moral and spiritual elements that have disappeared in recent decades. The time has come to look back on the virtues and values that made America great, not only in terms of its unmatched prosperity and affluence, or its military might, but in the breadth and depth of its moral leadership. To do so, we must instill fundamental virtues and values in the lives of the men and women, boys and girls of this land.

It was said of old, "Where the spirit of the Lord is, there is liberty" (2 Corinthians 3:17). And the Psalmist wrote, "The counsel of the Lord standeth for ever, the thoughts of his heart to all generations. Blessed is the nation whose God is the Lord" (Psalm 33:11–12).

We would do well to emphasize the kinds of virtues celebrated by the apostle Paul: "Whatsoever things are *true*, whatsoever things are *honest*, whatsoever things are *just*, whatsoever things are *pure*, whatsoever things are *lovely*, whatsoever things are of *good report*; if there be *any virtue*, and if there be any praise, think on these things. Those things, which ye have both learned, and received, and heard, and seen in me, do: and the God of peace shall be with you" (Philippians 4:8–9; emphasis added).

Values such as these, which form the roots of civility, flourish in homes where fathers and mothers, husbands and wives and children live together with love and appreciation and respect for one another. This is the way it was at Plymouth. This is the way it can and must be again, to keep America strong and robust, and to make its people happy as they look to the future. We as a people are at a time when we must openly embrace and celebrate the virtues for which we stand.

Even with the litany of problems that face us, there is still much strength in America. I am an optimist! I love this nation for its inherent greatness. I believe there is tremendous residual goodness in its people. For the most part, they appreciate that which is good and beautiful and uplifting. They acknowledge and appreciate values that lead to peace, goodwill, and behavior based on personal integrity. There has been a resurgent interest in things of a spiritual nature—another evidence of the inherently good instincts and longings of many people.

Men and women of all denominations have helped settle this land—Catholics and Protestants, Jews and Greeks, Muslims and Hindus. With few exceptions, those who helped establish this great country believed in and worshiped God, although their interpretations of Him may have varied.

They built for us a tremendous inheritance because they were men and women of faith and conviction. They had no government largesse to fall back on, but they looked to God in every extremity and thanked Him for every blessing.

Our great concern, our great interest, must be to preserve for the generations to come those wondrous elements of our society and manner of living that will bequeath to them the strengths and the goodness of which we have been the beneficiaries. To do so, we must retard and then halt the decay we observe about us, which comes of forsaking the God whom our forefathers knew, loved, worshiped, and looked to for strength.

Since the founding of this Republic, the roots of our nation have drawn nurture from the waters of faith in God. As we enter the twenty-first century, it is imperative that we renew our spiritual anchors. "God Bless America," we sing with reverence, pleading, and conviction. Future blessings will come only as we deserve them. Can we expect peace and prosperity, harmony and goodwill, when we turn our backs on the Source of our strength?

If we are to continue to have the freedoms that evolved within the structure that was the inspiration of the Almighty to our Founding Fathers, we must return to the God who is their true Author. We need to worship Him in spirit and in truth. We need to acknowledge His all-powerful hand. We need to humble ourselves before Him and seek His guidance. If we would individually and collectively resolve to stand for something, to lift our voices for truth and goodness and offer our supplications to our Eternal Father, those supplications would be heard, and the result would be remarkable.

Does this compromise the separation of church and state? Of course not. Such a provision does not preclude a constant petition to the Almighty for wisdom and guidance as we walk through perilous times.

Is it too much to expect that prayer, public and private, might once again be established in our national and private lives? Then, with a general acknowledgment of the God in whom we put our trust, we may expect a diminution in our social problems, an increase in public and private morality, and a renewed sense of freedom and liberty. I would hope that all of us, within our hearts, would then resolve to live nearer to God and the commandments He has given us as a guide in our lives; to walk with gratitude before Him for His generous mercies; to incorporate virtue in its many forms into our lives; to recognize that someday we all must give an accounting of our lives to Him; to strengthen and defend the home; and to seek His strength, His wisdom, His inspiration, and His love as we serve in the great society of which each of us is a part.

There is something reassuring about standing for something, and knowing what we stand for. For men or women who are true to themselves and to the virtues and standards they have personally adopted, it is not difficult to be true to others. Those who are committed to, and have patterned their lives after, a Higher Power need not rely on public opinion, which is often blatantly skewed.

Here is the answer to the conflicts that beset us. Here is the answer to the evils of pornography, abortion, drugs, and the squandering of our resources on evil pursuits. Here is the answer to the great epidemic of litigation that consumes time, saps our financial strength, and shackles our entrepreneurial spirit. Here is the answer to tawdry politics that place selfish interests and pursuits above the common good.

Let all houses of worship ring with righteousness. Let people everywhere bow in reverence before the Almighty who is our one true source of strength. Let us look inward and adjust our priorities and standards, recommitting ourselves to time-honored virtues that embrace right and shun wrong. Let us look outward in the spirit of the Golden Rule. Let us work tirelessly to defend and strengthen the family, which is the fundamental unit of society.

Notwithstanding the trouble, notwithstanding the argument, notwithstanding the increasingly heavy hand of government, notwithstanding the spirit of arrogance we so often display, notwithstanding the growing tide of pornography and permissiveness, notwithstanding corruption in public office and betrayal of sacred trust—I marvel at the miracle of America, the land which the God of Heaven long ago declared to be a choice land above all other lands, and at the people He has designated to inhabit this nation.

This is a good land, a great land with a glorious past and a bright future—if we treat and cure the sickness spreading throughout our society.

God bless America, for it is His creation.

PART ONE
The Ten Virtues

We need a new emphasis on honesty, character, and integrity. As we build into the fiber of our individual lives the virtues that are the essence of true civilization, so will the pattern of our times change. The question that confronts us is: Where shall we begin?

One

Love: The Lodestar of Life

Love is the only force that can erase the differences between people or bridge the chasms of bitterness.

When I was a little boy, we children traced paper hearts at school on Valentine's Day. At night, we dropped them at the doors of our friends, stamped on the porch, and then ran into the dark to hide.

Almost without exception, those Valentines had printed on them: "I love you." I have since come to know that love is more than a paper heart. Love is the very essence of life. It is the pot of gold at the end of the rainbow. Yet it is not found only at the end of the rainbow. Love is at the beginning also, and from it springs the beauty that arches across the sky on a stormy day. Love is the security for which children weep, the yearning of youth, the adhesive that binds marriage, and the lubricant that prevents devastating friction in the home; it is the peace of old age, the sunlight of hope shining through death. How rich are those who enjoy it in their associations with family, friends, and neighbors!

Love, like faith, is a gift of God. It is also the most enduring and most powerful virtue.

In our youth, we sometimes acquire faulty ideas of love, believing that it can be imposed or simply created for convenience. I noted the following in a newspaper column some years ago:

> One of the grand errors we tend to make when we are young is supposing that a person is a bundle of qualities, and we add up the individual's good and bad qualities, like a bookkeeper working on debits and credits. If the balance is favorable, we may decide to take the jump [into marriage]. . . . The world is full of unhappy men and women who married because . . . it seemed to be a good investment. Love, however, is not an investment; it is an adventure. And when marriage turns out to be as dull and comfortable as a sound investment, the disgruntled party soon turns elsewhere. . . . Ignorant people are always saying, "I wonder what he sees in her," not realizing that what he sees in her (and what no one else can see) is the secret essence of love.

I think of two friends from my high school and university years. He was a boy from a country town, plain in appearance, without money or apparent promise. He had grown up on a farm, and if he had any quality that was attractive, it was the capacity to work. He carried bologna sandwiches in a brown paper bag for his lunch, and swept the school floors to pay his tuition. But with all of his rustic appearance, he had a smile and a personality that seemed to sing of goodness. She was a city girl who had come out of a comfortable home. She would not have won a beauty contest, but she was wholesome in her decency and integrity, and attractive in her decorum and dress.

Something wonderful took place between them. They fell in love. Some whispered that there were far more promising boys for her, and a gossip or two noted that perhaps other girls might have interested him. But these two laughed and danced and studied together through their school years. They married when people wondered how they could ever earn enough to stay alive. He struggled through his professional school and came out well in his class. She scrimped and saved and worked and prayed. She encouraged and sustained, and when things were really tough, she said quietly, "Somehow we can make it." Buoyed by her faith in him, he kept going through the difficult years. Children came, and together they loved them and nourished them and gave them the security that came of their own love for and loyalty to each other. Now many years have passed. Their children are grown, a lasting credit to them and to the communities in which they live.

I happened to find myself on the same flight as this couple a few years ago. I walked down the aisle in the semidarkness of the cabin and saw a woman, white-haired, her head on her husband's shoulder as she dozed. His hand was clasped warmly about hers. He was awake and recognized me. She awakened, and we talked. They were returning from a convention where he had delivered a paper before a learned society. He said little about it, but she proudly spoke of the honors accorded him.

I wish that I might have caught with a camera the look on her face as she talked of him. Forty-five years earlier, people without understanding had asked what they saw in each other. I thought of that as I returned to my seat. Their friends of those days saw only a farm boy from the country and a smiling girl with freckles on her nose. But these two found in each other love and loyalty, peace and faith in the future. There was a flowering in them of something divine, planted there by that Father who is our God. In their school days, they had lived worthy of that flowering of love. They had lived with virtue and faith, with appreciation and respect for self and one another. In the years of their difficult professional and economic struggles, they had found their greatest earthly strength in their companionship. Now, in mature age, they were finding peace and quiet satisfaction together.

There is nothing as energizing, as confidence-building, as sustaining as the power of love. How substantial is its influence on the human mind and heart! How great and magnificent is its power in overcoming fear and doubt, worry and discouragement!

There are other great and necessary expressions of the gift of love. Consider the word of the Lord concerning the day of judgment when "the King [shall] say unto them on his right hand, Come, ye blessed of my Father, inherit the kingdom prepared for you from the foundation of the world: For I was an hungred, and ye gave me meat: I was thirsty, and ye gave me drink: I was a stranger, and ye took me in: naked, and ye clothed me: I was sick, and ye visited me: I was in prison, and ye came unto me.

"Then shall the righteous answer him, saying, Lord, when saw we thee an hungred, and fed thee? or thirsty, and gave thee drink? When saw we thee a stranger, and took thee in? or naked, and clothed thee? Or when saw we thee sick, or in prison, and came unto thee?

"And the King shall answer and say unto them, Verily I say unto you, Inasmuch as ye have done it unto one of the least of these my brethren, ye have done it unto me" (Matthew 25:34–40).

One of the greatest challenges we face in our hurried, self-centered lives is to follow this counsel of the Master, to take the time and make the effort to care for others, to develop and exercise the one quality that would enable us to change the lives of others—what the scriptures call *charity*.

We tend to think of charity as donations to a homeless shelter or a check written to a favorite institution that dispenses funds to those in need. But best defined, charity is that pure love exemplified by Jesus Christ. It embraces kindness, a reaching out to lift and help, the sharing of one's bread, if need be.

Consider Paul's great declaration: "Though I speak with the tongues of men and of angels, and have not charity, I am become as sounding brass, or a tinkling cymbal. And though I have the gift of prophecy, and understand all mysteries, and all knowledge; and though I have all faith, so that I could remove mountains, and have not charity, I am nothing. . . . Charity never faileth: but whether there be prophecies, they shall fail; whether there be tongues, they shall cease; whether there be knowledge, it shall vanish away" (1 Corinthians 13:1–2, 8).

The Master taught: "For whosoever will save his life shall lose it: but whosoever will lose his life for my sake, the same shall save it" (Luke 9:24).

This remarkable and miraculous process occurs in our own lives as we reach out with charity to serve others. Each of us can, with effort, successfully root the virtue of love deep in our beings so that we may be nourished by its great power all our lives. For it is as we tap into the power of love that we come to understand the great truth written by John: "God is love; and he that dwelleth in love dwelleth in God" (1 John 4:16).

Years ago, a young woman went into a rural area as a schoolteacher. Among those in her class was a girl who had failed before and who was failing again. The student could not read. She came from a family without the means to take her to a larger city for examination to determine whether she had a problem that could be remedied. Sensing that the difficulty might lie with the girl's eyes, the young teacher, at her own expense, arranged to take the student to have her eyes tested. A deficiency was discovered that could be corrected with glasses. With glasses, an entirely new world opened to the student. For the first time in her life, she saw clearly the words before her. The salary of that country schoolteacher was meager, but out of the little she had, she made an investment that completely changed the life of a failing student. In doing so, she found a new dimension in her own life.

Many of us can recount experiences in which we lost ourselves in the service of others and found those moments to be among the most rewarding of life. Everyone actively involved in serving God by reaching out to others can recount similar stories, as can devoted parents and marriage partners who have given of their time and means, who have loved and sacrificed so greatly that their concern for each other and for their children has known almost no bounds.

What a therapeutic and wonderful thing it is for a man or woman to set aside all consideration of personal gain and reach out with strength and energy and purpose to help the unfortunate, to improve and beautify the community, to clean up the environment. How much greater would be the suffering of the homeless and the hungry in our own communities without the service of hundreds of volunteers who give of their time and substance to assist them. All of us need to learn that life is a mission and not simply a career.

Tremendous happiness and peace of mind are the results of loving service to others. Nobody can live fully and happily who lives only unto himself or herself.

I was in North and South Vietnam not long ago. I made the trip because I wanted to return to the places I had visited during the war of the 1960s. In each city—in Ho Chi Minh City and in Hanoi—I found a handful of Americans who were teaching English, American doctors who were teaching and practicing medicine to relieve suffering, and others who were sharing their skills. One here, one there, giving service, loving it, and saying again and again, "It's the best thing I've ever done." It is as we serve, as we take time to express interest and concern in someone other than ourselves, that we are more likely to gain a glimpse of who we really are and what we can ultimately become.

Around the corner from Trafalgar Square in London stands a beautiful statue of an English girl. On that statue are engraved the words, "Brussels Dawn, 1918," and, "Patriotism is not enough, I must have love for all men." The statue celebrates the heroism of Edith Cavell, who was shot by German conquerors in Brussels as an English spy, although she was there working as a nurse doing Christian good. I first saw that statue over sixty years ago, and the impact of its message has stayed with me: "Patriotism is not enough, I must have love for all men."

Love is the only force that can erase the differences between people or bridge the chasms of bitterness. I think frequently of these lines by Edwin Markham, which in simple terms endorse the virtue of reaching out with love and kindness to those who would revile against us:

> He drew a circle that shut me out—
> Heretic, rebel, a thing to flout.
> But Love and I had the wit to win:
> We drew a circle that took him in!

He who most beautifully taught this everlasting truth was the Son of God, the one perfect exemplar, teacher, and embodiment of love. His coming to earth was an expression of His Father's love. "For God so loved the world, that he gave his only begotten Son, that whosoever believeth in him should not perish, but have everlasting life. For God sent not his Son into the world to condemn the world; but that the world through him might be saved" (John 3:16–17). In the ultimate expression of love, He did something for us that we could not do for ourselves.

Now, to all of us who would be His disciples, He has given the great commandment, "A new commandment I give unto you, That ye love one another; as I have loved you, that ye also love one another" (John 13:34).

If the world is to be improved, the process of love must make a change in the hearts of humans. It can do so when we look beyond self to give our love to God and others, and do so with all our hearts, with all our souls, and with all our minds.

As we look with love and gratitude to God, and as we serve others with no apparent recompense for ourselves, there will come a greater sense of service toward our fellow human beings, less thinking of self and more reaching out to others. This principle of love is the basic essence of goodness.

When I was a boy, we lived on a farm in the summer. It was in the country, where the nights were dark. There were no streetlights or anything of the kind. My brother and I slept outdoors. On clear nights—in those days, most of the nights were clear and the air was clean—we would lie on our backs and look at the myriads of stars in the heavens. We could identify some of the constellations and other stars that were illustrated in our encyclopedia. Each night, we would trace the Big Dipper, the handle and the cup, to find the North Star.

We came to know of the constancy of that star. As the earth turned, the others appeared to move through the night. But the North Star held its position in line with the axis of the earth. And so it had come to be known as the Polar Star—the Polestar, or the Lodestar. Through centuries of time, mariners had used it to guide them in their journeys. They had reckoned their bearings by its constancy, thereby avoiding traveling in circles or in the wrong direction as they moved across the wide, unmarked seas.

Because of those boyhood musings, the Polar Star came to mean something to me. I recognized it as a constant in the midst of change. It was something that could always be counted on, something that was dependable, an anchor in what otherwise appeared to be a moving and unstable firmament.

Love is like the Polar Star. In a changing world, it is a constant. It is something that, when sincere, never moves. It is the very essence of the teachings of Christ. It is the security of the home. It is the safeguard of community life. It is a beacon of hope in a world of distress.

As we look across the broad spectrum of humanity and see the masses who walk in hunger and poverty and who suffer the constant afflictions of disease and misery, let us be generous with our substance to assist.

Let love become the lodestar of our lives in reaching out to those who need our strength. There are many among us who live in pain—emotional and spiritual pain as well as physical hardship. There are many who walk in frightening circum-stances, fearful and unable to cope alone. It was said of the Savior that He "went about doing good" (Acts 10:38). He is the supreme model for each of us.

Said Isaiah, "Strengthen ye the weak hands, and confirm the feeble knees. Say to them that are of a fearful heart, Be strong, fear not: behold, your God will come with vengeance, even God with a recompense; he will come and save you" (Isaiah 35:3–4).

Such are the injunctions—these and many more—to reach out to those in distress with a measure of the love epito-mized by the life and works of the Savior.

Admittedly, it is not always easy to follow the Polar Star of love. It requires a discipline almost beyond the power of many to observe. I think it is the most difficult and also the most important of all commandments. But out of its observance come a remarkable discipline and a refining influence that are wonderful to experience.

Few of us see the Polar Star anymore. We live in urban centers, and the city lights affect our vision of the wondrous firmament above us. But, as it has been for centuries, the star is there in its place; its constancy is a guide and an anchor. So likewise is love—unyielding and unchanging.

The virtue of love changes lives—ours as well as those of everyone with whom we come in contact. It is the virtue that has embedded within its precincts the power to have the most lasting good.

Where There Is *Honesty,* Other Virtues Will Follow

In our day, those found in dishonesty aren't put to death, but something within them dies. Conscience chokes, character withers, self-respect vanishes, integrity dies. How cheaply some men and women sell their good names!

The year my schoolmates and I enrolled in junior high, the building could not accommodate all of the students, and it was determined that our seventh-grade class would be sent back to our old grade school.

We were insulted. We were furious. We'd spent six years in that grade-school building, and we were ready to move on. We were above going to school one more year with the younger grades. We felt we deserved something better. As a result of this perceived insult, we boys of the class all met after school. We decided that we wouldn't tolerate this kind of treatment and that we should show our displeasure by going on strike.

The next day, we did not show up for school. But we had no place to go. We couldn't stay home because our mothers would ask questions. We didn't think of going downtown to a show because we had no money for that. We didn't think of going to the park where we might be seen by the truant officer. We didn't think of going out behind the school fence and telling shady stories because, to be honest, we didn't know any. We had never heard of such things as drugs or anything of that kind. So we just wandered about and wasted the day.

The next morning, the principal, Mr. Stearns, whose demeanor matched the sound of his name, was at the front door of the grade school to greet us as we entered. He said some fairly straightforward things and then told us that we could not come back to school until we brought a note from our parents. That was my first experience with a lockout. Striking, he said, was not the way to settle a problem. We were expected to be responsible citizens, and if we had a complaint, we could come to the principal's office and discuss it. There was only one thing to do: go home and get the note.

I will never forget walking sheepishly into the house. Mother was, of course, surprised to see me and asked what was wrong. I told her what I had done and explained that I needed a note. She wrote this brief note, the most stinging rebuke she ever gave me:

Dear Mr. Stearns,

> Please excuse Gordon's absence yesterday. His action was simply an impulse to follow the crowd.

I have never forgotten my mother's note. Neither I nor my friends ever tried that tactic again. From our parents and principal we learned that there are proper avenues for settling grievances, and that the fundamental problem with our act had been the deception involved. I resolved then and there that I would never do anything in which I was simply following the crowd. I determined that I would make my own decisions on the basis of their merits and my standards, and would not be pushed in one direction or another by those around me. And I also determined that I would be honest and would never again resort to deception.

That decision has blessed me many times, sometimes in very uncomfortable circumstances. It has kept me from doing some things that might have resulted in serious injury and trouble, and, at the very least, would have cost me my self-respect and integrity. It has helped me be true to what I believe and honest with myself and with others. I have often quietly thanked my mother for the rebuke that had such influence on me as a young seventh-grade boy.

As schoolboys, my friends and I were far from perfect. We were not very good athletes, but we were determined in our competition. We had fistfights with one another until our noses ran with blood. But so far as I am able to ascertain, no boy in that class was ever arrested for anything worse than a traffic violation. All went on to higher study and productive lives. How grateful I am for the values we were taught, for the discipline that was expected of us, for parents who pointed out a better way to live.

Some may regard the quality of character known as honesty to be an unspectacular virtue and an ordinary, pedestrian topic for contemplation and consideration. In recent years, we have been subjected to widespread public debate about the seriousness of lying. The apparent number of citizens who seem remarkably unconcerned about major breaches of trust by public figures has been disheartening and surprising. Our eroding moral climate is serious not merely in the present but in its ramifications for future leaders and generations.

Fraudulent insurance claims, padded expense accounts, bogus checks, forged documents—these are all symptomatic of an epidemic of unbelievable proportions. In most instances, the amount involved individually is small, but in total it represents personal dishonesty on a huge scale.

Falsehood is not new. It is as old as humanity. "The Lord said unto Cain, Where is Abel thy brother? And he said, I know not: Am I my brother's keeper?" (Genesis 4:9). This was, of course, the first known attempt to conceal the taking of innocent life.

In our day, dishonesty does not always revolve around such a grievous offense, nor are those found in dishonesty put to death for their misdeeds, as in biblical times. But something within them dies. Conscience chokes, character withers, self-respect vanishes, integrity dies.

Without honesty, our lives disintegrate into ugliness, chaos, and a lack of any kind of security and confidence. Imagine a society in which it would be unwise or unsafe to trust anyone—from elected officials to financial advisers to insurance adjusters to your child's babysitter or kindergarten teacher. Imagine having surgery performed by someone who had cheated in medical school or found a way to short-circuit the requirements of medical residency. Imagine the terror of a society that condones or at least turns a collective blind eye to dishonesty. The prospects are horrifying!

Among many letters I have received from anonymous senders was one that contained a twenty-dollar bill and a brief note stating that the writer had come to my home many years ago. When there had been no response to the bell, he had tried the door and, finding it unlocked, had entered and walked about. On the dresser he saw a twenty-dollar bill, which he took. Through the years, his conscience had bothered him, and he was now returning the money.

He did not include any amount for interest for the period during which he had used my money. But as I read his pathetic letter, I thought of the usury to which he had subjected himself for a quarter of a century: the unceasing nagging of his conscience. For him, there had been no peace until he had made restitution.

A local paper carried a similar story. The state of Utah received an unsigned note that read: "The enclosed is for materials used over the years I worked for the state—envelopes, paper, stamps, etc." Enclosed was two hundred dollars.

Imagine the flood of money that would pour into the offices of government, business, and merchants if all who had filched a little here and a little there were to return that which they had dishonestly taken.

The cost of every bag of groceries, of every tie or blouse, includes a percentage to cover the burden of shoplifting and "shrinkage," as retailers refer to it today. Each time we board a plane, we pay a premium so that our persons and our baggage may be searched in the interest of security. In the aggregate, this amounts to millions of dollars, all because of the frightening dishonesty of a few who, by threat and blackmail, would try to obtain that to which they are not entitled, or whose lack of integrity and common decency tempts them to injure or threaten others for personal gain.

We are barraged with vivid displays of dishonesty on the nightly news. The media parade before us a veritable procession of deception in its many ugly forms.

What was once controlled by the moral and ethical standards of the people, we now seek to handle by public law—and there is even debate among the keepers of that law. And so the statutes multiply, enforcement agencies consume ever-increasing billions, and prison facilities are constantly expanded—but the torrent of dishonesty pours on and grows in volume.

How cheaply some men and women sell their good names! The case of a prominent figure who was arrested for taking an item costing less than five dollars was widely publicized. The legal outcome of his case is almost insignificant; his petty misdeed convicted him before the people, particularly his colleagues, his friends, and, most importantly, his family. In a measure, his foolish act nullified much of the good he had done and was capable of still doing. Once the stain of dishonesty has disfigured a man or woman, it is difficult to remove the resultant lingering doubt and distrust. Said Shakespeare through his character Iago: "Good name in man and woman, . . . is the immediate jewel of their souls; who steals my purse steals trash, . . . but he that filches from me my good name robs me of that which not enriches him and makes me poor indeed."

And yet, not long ago, on a popular radio call-in show in Salt Lake City, the host said at least two dozen times, "*No one is honest every day.*"

Such a blanket indictment is not only unbelievable, it is insulting! There are still people in this world—we can only hope they are many in number—who are impeccably honest, day in and day out. People who do what they say they will do. People whose word is equal to any bond.

I will never forget a train ride my wife, Marjorie, and I took from Osaka to Nagoya, Japan. Friends were waiting to greet us at the station in Nagoya, and, in the excitement, Marj left her purse on the train. When we discovered it was missing, we immediately called the Tokyo station, where the train was headed, to report the loss. But we had little hope that the purse would be found. Much to our delight, however, when the train arrived in Tokyo three hours later, a railroad official telephoned to say the purse was there on the seat where Marj had left it. We were not returning via Tokyo, so he promised to send it to us in the United States. Again, our expectations were low. More than a month passed. But then, one day, to our surprise, it arrived at our home in Salt Lake City. The purse and all of its contents, including the Japanese yen, were intact.

Integrity is at the heart of commerce in the world in which we live. Honesty and integrity comprise the very underpinnings of society. Every bank president, every bank director knows that even with all of the regulations and possible safeguards, in the last analysis the strength and safety of any financial institution lie in the integrity of its people. As with banks, so also with merchants, politicians, professional men and women, and leaders from all walks of life. Indeed, the strength and safety of *any* organization—including the family—lie in the integrity of its members. Without personal integrity, there can be no confidence. Without confidence, there can be no prospect of permanent success.

I have always been fascinated by Lloyd's of London, which has the reputation of being the ultimate underwriter of possible catastrophes. I was even more impressed, however, after reading an article that described this company's business philosophy:

> The costs of a hijacking, recovering from major disasters like earthquakes, . . . [and so forth] almost invariably come home to Lloyd's. The size and nature of the risks make the comparatively simple way Lloyd's works all the more impressive. For Lloyd's is not a company—it has no shareholders and accepts no corporate liability for risks insured there. It is a society of individual underwriters, and it works like a market. Its existence is built on two principles: That of the utter integrity of everyone who belongs to Lloyd's and does business there, and that of unlimited personal liability.

Leadership—of the family, an organization, our society, or even the nation—erodes and eventually falls apart without honesty and integrity. Honesty is the keystone that holds any organization together. Tom Peters, in his landmark management treatise *In Search of Excellence*, reported that the most successful businesses were those that focused internally on integrity. He summarized, "Without doubt, honesty has always been the best policy."

Codes and covenants, promises and principles, are as old as humanity and as contemporary as marriage. And they are the very foundation of a secure, united, and prosperous society.

Athens was once recognized as the greatest city in the then-known world. It was a seat not only of Greece's government but of learning and commerce, of art and science. Each young man of Athens, when he reached the age of eighteen, took this oath:

We will never bring disgrace on this our City by an act of dishonesty or cowardice.

We will fight for the ideals and sacred things of the City, both alone and with many.

We will revere and obey the City's laws, and will do our best to incite a like reverence and respect in those above us who are prone to annul them or set them at naught.

We will strive increasingly to quicken the public sense of civic duty.

Thus in all these ways we will transmit this City, not lessened, but greater and more beautiful than it was transmitted to us.

That solemn commitment, and its subsequent expression in the lives of the young men of Athens, became the foundation of the principles and behavior that made Athens the cultural capital of the world. Codes of behavior are not new, nor are they out-of-date.

Presidents of our nation, justices of the Supreme Court, our legislators, and public officers serving at many levels raise their arm to the square and solemnly pledge to uphold the laws of the land and to prosecute their responsibilities with fidelity and honor.

The marriage ceremony of many faiths is a covenant made in solemnity.

All of us who are citizens of this nation salute the flag and pledge our allegiance to it and to the nation for which it stands.

Jehovah made a covenant with Abraham and his posterity that He would be their God and they would be His people.

It is surely neither coincidence nor happenstance that five of the Ten Commandments deal essentially with honesty in its broadest sense. "Thou shalt not kill" (Exodus 20:13). It is an act of the most grievous kind of dishonesty and betrayal to take the life of another. "Thou shalt not steal" (Exodus 20:15). Stealing is obviously an act of dishonesty. It covers the whole broad range of theft, from cheating and plagiarism to lying, deceit, and taking to oneself that which belongs to another. It is reprehensible, inexcusable, and a violation of a standard of conduct that lies at the bedrock of civilization.

"Thou shalt not commit adultery" (Exodus 20:14). Was there ever adultery without rank dishonesty? In the vernacular, this evil is described as "cheating." And cheating it is, for it robs virtue, it robs loyalty, it robs sacred promises, it robs truth. It involves deception. It is personal dishonesty of the most selfish, insulting kind, for it becomes a betrayal of the most sacred of human relationships and a denial of covenants and promises entered into before God and society. It is the sordid violation of a trust. It is a selfish casting aside of the law of God, and, as with other forms of dishonesty, its fruits are sorrow, bitterness, heartbroken companions, and betrayed children. It is nothing less than the theft of sacred marriage vows and promises.

"Thou shalt not bear false witness against thy neighbour" (Exodus 20:16). The malicious spreading of untrue accusations in an effort to injure another is the most vicious kind of dishonesty.

A news program recently reported on a woman imprisoned unjustly for twenty-seven years. She had been convicted on the testimony of witnesses who later came forth to confess that they had lied. I realize that this is an extreme case, but are we not all acquainted with instances of reputations damaged, of hearts broken, of careers destroyed by the lying tongues of those who have borne false witness?

I recall a book of history, a long and detailed account of the trickeries practiced by the nations involved in World War II. The theme of the book is taken from these words of Winston Churchill: "In war-time, truth is so precious that she should always be attended by a bodyguard of lies." The book deals with the many deceptions practiced on each side of the conflict. Reading it, one is again led to the conclusion that war is the devil's own game and that among its most precious victims is truth.

Unfortunately, the easy use of falsehood and deception, rationalized and exploited during war by military strategists, goes on long after the treaties of peace are signed. Some of those schooled in the art of lying during battle find it difficult to disengage from what has become a comfortable kind of dishonesty, and they continue to ply their skills in days of peace. Then, like a disease that is endemic, the evil spreads and grows in virulence.

"Thou shalt not covet." Is not covetousness—that dishonest, cankering evil—the root of most of the world's sorrows? Coveting partakes of the greedy desire to have that which belongs to another. It is evil because it leads to evil consequences.

For what a tawdry price people of avarice barter their lives! I recall a sequence of unfortunate events involving the leaders of a prominent financial institution. After the death of the president, a senior vice president competed to replace him. He had always been an honorable and able man, but in his avarice to get ahead, he compromised principle after principle until he was utterly destroyed. In the process, he almost took down to ruin the very institution he had sought to lead. The histories of business, of government, of institutions of many kinds are replete with instances of covetous persons who in their selfish, dishonest, upward climb destroyed others and eventually destroyed themselves. Good persons, well-intentioned persons of great capacity, trade character for trinkets that then turn to wax before their eyes. Their dreams become haunting nightmares. Dishonesty does not pay—not now, not ever.

Everyone wants to be successful. The question is: Successful at what? Successful at earning money, successful in marriage, successful in our own sight and in the eyes of our friends? None of these aspirations is necessarily wrong. But greed is an insidious trap that has the power to destroy those whose eager search for success becomes the driving force of their lives. Greed is the devious, sinister, evil influence that makes people say, "What I have is not enough. I must have more. And I will do whatever it takes to get it."

When I first heard the word *yuppie*, I did not know what it meant. I subsequently learned that it generally referred to a generation of young, mostly well-educated people who with careful design set out on a course to get rich, drive fancy automobiles, wear the best of clothing, have a condominium in New York and a home in the country, and more. This course was the total end for which they lived; for some, how they got there, in terms of ethics and morality, was unimportant. They coveted the lifestyle that others had, and selfishness and greed were part of their process of acquisitiveness.

How wonderful it would be if everyone were to succeed in his or her appropriate pursuits! But we must be careful about how we measure success. One need only read the daily newspapers to see case after case of those whose driving, greedy impulses have led to trouble, not to mention serious and abysmal failure. Some of those who once drove about in the fanciest of cars and owned the fanciest of homes are now languishing in prison. They were people who had tremendous capacity and ability, but, in many cases, their brilliance led to their downfall. During the past few years, an alarming number of individuals began working with integrity and honesty and lived in reasonable comfort, but they were not satisfied. In their greed to enlarge their own kingdom, they enticed others to invest with them. And those who invested in their enterprises, in many cases, were also plagued with the affliction of greed. They listened to stories of large returns with little effort. Like a dog chasing its own tail, the momentum of the scheme increased until one day there was a collapse. Both the promoter and the investor were left only with shattered dreams. What had been a friendly and pleasant association became one of accusation and meanness, if not criminal prosecution and attempts to recover losses through civil litigation.

There have been many changes in the world since the finger of the Lord gave as the tenth and final commandment: "Thou shalt not covet thy neighbour's house, thou shalt not covet thy neighbour's wife, nor his manservant, nor his maidservant, nor his ox, nor his ass, nor any thing that is thy neighbour's" (Exodus 20:17). But human nature has not changed.

In one of his great letters to Timothy, Paul wrote: "For the love of money is the root of all evil: which while some coveted after, they have erred from the faith, and pierced themselves through with many sorrows" (1 Timothy 6:10). Money itself is not evil. It is the relentless pursuit of wealth at the expense of everything else—including personal integrity and valor— that too often leads to debauchery. We need not look far to see the veritable truth of that profound warning. Once made rich through a consuming desire for money, these people of whom I speak now find themselves "pierced . . . through with many sorrows."

I think of a friend who was a good man. He had a good home and a good family, and plenty to take care of his needs and the needs of his family. But he became consumed by a yearning for greater riches. One thing led to another until a drop in the economy occurred, and he found himself in a trap from which he could not extricate himself. Those who wanted him to make them rich, and who initially professed love for him and admiration for his business acumen, became his violent and hateful accusers. It was not the money itself that destroyed them. It was the love of money that took hold of them and drove them until they found themselves in difficulty and failure.

Of course, we need to earn a living. The Lord told Adam that in the sweat of his face should he eat his bread all the days of his life. It is important that we qualify ourselves to be self-reliant, particularly that every young man, at the time of marriage, be ready and able to assume the responsibilities of providing for his partner and for the children that may come to that home. This is important. It is wholesome. It is right and proper.

Whatever our circumstances, we want to improve them. This is good if it is not carried to an extreme. I am satisfied that the Father of us all does not wish His children to walk in poverty. He wants the best for us. He wants us to enjoy the good things of the earth. In the Old Testament, He speaks of "a land flowing with milk and honey," of the fatlings of the flock, and of other things that indicate He would have His children properly fed and clothed and sheltered, enjoying the comforts that come of the earth.

It is when greed takes over, when we covet that which others have, that our affliction begins. And it can be a very sore and painful affliction if it invites us to compromise our integrity because of a "do-whatever-it-takes" attitude. If we buy into the marketers of Madison Avenue, with their slick advertising campaigns that promote the good life and entice us with the baubles of an affluent society without ever mentioning how to pay for them, none of us will ever feel that we have enough.

"Thou shalt not covet thy neighbour's house." We all need shelter. We all need a roof over our heads with warmth in the winter and a measure of comfort in the summer. But when we go to wild excess, as many are prone to do, including those who are young, our folly can become as a trap to destroy us.

Thou shalt not covet thy neighbor's car. The modern automobile is wonderful and almost indispensable in the society in which we live and work. But when I see relatively young people borrowing heavily to buy cars costing tens of thousands of dollars, I wonder what has happened to our values. I wonder about our priorities. I wonder about what appears to be an alarming absence of common sense.

It is so with boats and other fancy toys. When one family in a neighborhood gets a boat, the others think they need one too. To satisfy our desires, we go into debt, dissipate our resources in the payment of high interest, and become like indentured servants working to pay off our debts. Please do not misunderstand me: I wish everyone might have some of the good things of life. But I hope our desires will not come of covetousness and greed, which together form an evil and gnawing disease.

How rare a gem, how precious a jewel is the man or woman in whom there is neither guile nor deception nor falsehood nor greed nor a preoccupation with "getting ahead." The appraisal spoken long ago by Alexander Pope, the English poet, is true yet today: "An honest man's the noblest work of God." Why is honesty so vital? Because where honesty and integrity are present, other virtues follow. And conversely, where there are serious breaches of integrity, they are almost always accompanied by other moral lapses.

Wrote the author of Proverbs: "These six things doth the Lord hate: yea, seven are an abomination unto him: A proud look, a lying tongue, and hands that shed innocent blood, a heart that deviseth wicked imaginations, feet that be swift in running to mischief, a false witness that speaketh lies, and he that soweth discord among brethren" (Proverbs 6:16–19).

The moniker "Honest Abe" is one that Abraham Lincoln apparently deserved and earned, and throughout his life he was disturbed when he encountered individuals who could not be trusted. At one critical point during the Civil War, it came to his attention that some of his trusted Union officers were giving key pieces of information to Confederate leaders.

Lincoln was admittedly distressed at this lack of loyalty among self-proclaimed Union supporters. During one meeting in particular, his Secretary of War presented evidence condemning several of these individuals as traitors, and then asked the President what he wished for him to do. Lincoln, who had remained silent through the presentation, then shared his feelings by telling the story of a farmer who loved a large shade tree that stood as a sentinel near his house:

> It was a majestic-looking tree, and apparently perfect in every part—tall, straight. . . . One morning, while at work in his garden, [the farmer] saw a squirrel [run up the tree into a hole] and thought the tree might be hollow. He proceeded to examine it carefully and, much to his surprise, he found that the stately [tree] that he had [valued] for its beauty and grandeur to be the pride and protection of his little farm was hollow from top to bottom. Only a rim of sound wood remained, barely sufficient to support its weight. What was he to do? If he cut it down, it would [do great damage] with its great length and spreading branches. If he let it remain, his family was in constant danger. In a storm it might fall, or the wind might blow it down, and his house and children be crushed by it. What should he do? As he turned away, he said sadly: "I wish I had never seen that squirrel."

Very simply, we cannot be less than honest, we cannot be less than true, we cannot be less than virtuous if we are to keep sacred the trust given us by those who have gone before us, or if we are to merit the trust and confidence of those with whom we live, work, and associate. Once it was said among our people that a man's word was as good as his bond. Shall any of us be less reliable, less honest than our forebears? Those who are dishonest with others canker their own souls and soon learn that they cannot trust even themselves.

I once overheard a man—a strong and wise man whom I admired greatly—gently counsel his daughter, who was leaving on a date: "Be careful. Be careful of how you act and what you say."

"Daddy, don't you trust me?" she quickly asked.

"I don't entirely trust myself," he responded. "One never gets so old or so wise that the adversary gives up on him."

Each of us must keep faith with ourselves and with others. So many of us begin strong and then flatten out. So many players in the game of life get to first base. Some reach second. A handful make third. But how few there are who reach home base safely. It requires continual striving to gain that mastery over self. As Henry Wadsworth Longfellow observed:

> The heights by great men reached and kept
> Were not attained by sudden flight,
> But they, while their companions slept,
> Were toiling upward in the night.

Karl G. Maeser, an educator from Germany, served as the first president of Brigham Young University, now the largest private, church-owned university in the United States. More than a century ago, he said this to his students: "I have been asked what I mean by 'word of honor.' I will tell you. Place me behind prison walls—walls of stone ever so high, ever so thick, reaching ever so far into the ground—there is a possibility that in some way or another I might be able to escape; but stand me on the floor and draw a chalk line around me and have me give my word of honor never to cross it. Can I get out of that circle? No, never! I'd die first."

Can we not, as we enter the twenty-first century, vow to keep faith with the best that is in us? Can we not reenthrone the twin virtues of integrity and honesty? It *is* possible to be honest every day. It *is* possible to live so that others can trust us—can trust our words, our motives, and our actions. Our examples are vital to those who sit at our feet as well as those who watch from a distance. Our own constant self-improvement will become as a polar star to those within our individual spheres of influence. They will remember longer what they *saw* in us than what they *heard* from us. Our attitude, our point of view, can make a tremendous difference.

My father told me, when I was a boy, a story that I have never forgotten. An older boy and his young companion were walking along a road that led through a field. They saw an old coat and a badly worn pair of men's shoes by the roadside, and, in the distance, they saw the owner working in the field. The younger boy suggested that they hide the shoes, conceal themselves, and watch the perplexity on the owner's face when he returned. The older boy, a benevolent lad, thought that would not be so good. He said the owner must be a very poor man. After discussing the matter, they concluded to try another experiment. Instead of hiding the shoes, they would put a silver dollar in each one and, concealing themselves, see what the owner did when he discovered the money.

Soon the man returned from the field, put on his coat, slipped one foot into a shoe, felt something hard, took it out, and found a silver dollar. Wonder and surprise showed in his face. He looked at the dollar again and again, turned around and could see nobody, then proceeded to put on the other shoe where, to his great surprise, he found another dollar. His feelings overcame him and he knelt down and offered aloud a prayer of thanksgiving, in which he spoke of his wife being sick and helpless and his children without bread. Then he fervently thanked the Lord for this bounty from unknown hands and evoked the blessing of heaven upon those who had given him this needed help. The boys remained concealed until he had gone. Then they quietly walked along the lane and one said to the other, "Don't you have a good feeling? Aren't you glad we didn't try to deceive him?"

Men and women of integrity understand intrinsically that theirs is the precious right to hold their heads in the sunlight of truth, unashamed before anyone. Embodied within this simple principle and character trait rests the foundational virtue of every person and of every society.

Three

Making a Case for *Morality*

Both experience and divine wisdom dictate that moral virtue and cleanliness pave the way that leads to strength of character, peace of mind and heart, and happiness in life.

I once had a conversation with a young man in a South American airport, where both of our planes were delayed. His hair was unkempt and his face bearded; his glasses were large and round. His clothing gave the appearance of total indifference to any generally accepted standard or style. But he was earnest and evidently sincere, educated, and thoughtful. Without employment, and sustained by his father, he was traveling throughout South America.

What was he after in life? I asked. "Peace—and freedom," was his immediate response. Did he use drugs? Yes, they were one of his means to obtaining the peace and freedom he sought. The discussion of drugs led to a discussion of morals. He talked matter-of-factly about modern morality, which gave him, he felt, much more freedom than any previous generation had ever known.

He had learned in our opening introductions that I was a religious leader. He let me know, in something of a condescending way, that he regarded the morality of my generation, and all those preceding it, a joke. Then, with earnestness, he asked how I could honestly defend personal virtue and moral chastity. I shocked him when I declared that *his* freedom was a delusion, that *his* peace was a fraud, that they would be bought at great personal and social cost, and that I would tell him why.

Our flights were called shortly after that, and we had to separate. Since then, I have thought much of that discussion. I wish we had had time to finish our conversation. He represents a generation numbered in the millions who, in search of freedom from moral restraint and peace from a guilty conscience, have sought to legitimize, even celebrate practices that enslave and debauch and, if left unchecked, will destroy not only individuals but also the nations of which they are a part.

It is virtually impossible today to shield ourselves from immoral influences. Our culture is saturated with them. Adultery, fornication, homosexuality, pornography—they all wreak their own brands of spiritual devastation, all in the name of freedom and peace.

I thought of this so-called freedom when I spoke with a young man and woman in my office. He was handsome, tall, and talented. She was a beautiful girl, an excellent student, sensitive, and perceptive.

The girl sobbed, and tears fell from the eyes of the young man. They were university students and were to be married the following week. But it would not be the kind of wedding they had dreamed of. It would not come as the culmination of their planning and preparation. Instead, it would be hurried. It would interrupt their studies and their dreams, a situation which both regretted and for which neither was prepared—emotionally or in any other way. Shattered were their plans for schooling, the years of preparation they knew each needed for the competitive world that lay ahead. Rather, they would have to interrupt their studies to establish a home. He would become the breadwinner at the best figure his meager skills could command. The young man looked up through his tears. "We were sold short," he lamented.

"We've cheated one another," she responded. "We've cheated one another and the parents who love us—and we've cheated ourselves. We have betrayed ourselves." She explained how they had fallen for the rubbish that virtue is hypocrisy. They had found that the lack of moral standards, which permeates television and the movies and the culture in general, was a booby trap that destroyed them.

They spoke of a thousand doubts and fears that had played across their minds during the anxious days and nights of the past few weeks. Should she seek an abortion? The temptation was there in the frightening contemplation of the ordeal that lay ahead of her—the awkwardness of her situation and the embarrassment she would suffer. It seemed like a way around the consequences, but would it soothe the anguish that plagued her? No, she had concluded; never would she take an innocent life that she had helped create. Life was sacred under any circumstance. She knew she could never live with herself if she took measures to destroy this gift of life, even in this unfortunate predicament.

Likewise, he had decided to be responsible—he would never leave her to face this trial alone. He would meet his responsibility even though it blighted the future of which he had dreamed. I admired their courage and their determination to make the best of a difficult situation, but my heart ached as I watched them. Here was tragedy. Here was bondage. They had bartered their inner peace and freedom—the freedom to marry when they chose to marry, the freedom to secure the education of which they had dreamed, and, more importantly, the peace of self-respect.

My young friend in the airport might have countered my story by saying they were not smart. Had they been wise to the means available to them, they would not have found themselves in this sorry situation. I would have replied that their situation is far from unique.

The violation of moral virtues in this age, as in any other age, brings only regret, sorrow, loss of self-respect, and, in many cases, tragedy. Rationalization and equivocation will not erase the cankering scar that blights the self-respect of a man or woman who gives away that virtue which can never be replaced. Self-justification will never mend the hearts of those who have drifted into moral tragedy.

Right is right and wrong is wrong.

According to a 1997 nationwide survey, divorce is 32 percent more likely among those who engaged in premarital sex than it is among the general population. And almost three times as many separated or divorced Americans have committed adultery, compared to the general population. Further, 82 percent of adults who rate their marriage as "very strong" (9 or 10 on a 10-point scale) did not engage in premarital sex. This should not surprise us. Immorality is a breach of integrity of the highest order. On the other hand, those who have demonstrated sexual purity are also likely to have cultivated other moral virtues that contribute to the success of any relationship, particularly marriage. Each of us has the capacity to control his or her own thoughts and actions. This is part of the process of developing spiritual, physical, and emotional maturity.

Self-discipline is not necessarily easy. It requires effort and strength. It requires thought and prayer. In the long run, however, self-discipline is a far easier path than is blatant indulgence, which leads to a corrosion of heart and spirit.

In the 1960s, I visited Korea dozens of times. I saw the tragic aftermath of war, not just in the loss of life and destruction of property but in the thousands of orphans born of Korean mothers and American soldier fathers. These children were largely abandoned. They were unwanted creatures of sorrow, the flotsam of a miserable tide of immorality.

It was the same in Vietnam. Tens of thousands of interracial children were produced during that war. Peace and freedom? There can be neither for the men who wantonly indulged nor for the children left as the innocent and tragic victims of their lust. Any self-justification is only self-deception and a miserable fraud. It was said of old that "he that governeth himself is greater than he that taketh a city." Can there really be peace in the heart or freedom in the life of any man who has left only misery as the bitter fruit of his indulgence? Can anything be more false or dishonest than gratification of passion without acceptance of responsibility?

One evening, as I thumbed through the newspaper, I came upon the theater ads. So many of them openly appealed to readers to expose themselves to debauchery. I turned to my mail, found a small magazine that lists the television fare for the coming week, and saw titles of shows aimed in the same direction. A news magazine lay on my desk. That particular issue was devoted to the rising crime rate, with emphasis on the degrading influence and high cost of pornography, drugs, and gangs. Articles in the magazine spoke of the additional billions needed for expanded police forces, more juvenile and drug rehab centers, and larger prisons.

Our legislatures and courts are affected by this wave. Legal restraints against immoral behavior are eroding under legislative enactments and court opinions. This is done in the name of freedom—freedom of speech, freedom of the press, freedom of choice in so-called personal matters. But the abuse of these freedoms has yielded enslavement to degrading habits, and behavior that leads only to destruction.

Michael Medved's book *Hollywood vs. America* paints a gloomy picture of the miserable and dark obsession with sex among many television and movie producers. He refers to the "Hollywood dream factory" as a "poison factory," and quotes a 1990 Associated Press/Media General poll in which 80 percent of Americans objected to the amount of foul language in motion pictures; 82 percent, to the amount of violence; and 72 percent, to the amount of explicit sexuality. The producers of this trash are out of step with the feelings of mainstream America. But in their obsession, they are without doubt influencing and leading millions down a course that invites all too many to readjust their personal moral standards.

In the old film *International Hotel,* W.C. Fields was flying through the clouds when he noticed that his supply of beer was running out. He landed on the roof of the International Hotel somewhere in China, where the elite of the city were gathered for afternoon tea. Fields asked where he was. "Wu Hu," came the reply. "I'm looking for Kansas City, Kansas," he announced. "You are lost, sir!" someone responded. Whereupon, with something of arrogance and conceit, he raised his head, threw out his chest, and said, "Kansas City is lost; I am here!"

So it is with the writers and producers of the insipid, destructive programming that jams the airwaves. In their egotism, they consider it their mission to educate America concerning its morals. Several years ago, a prominent television producer boasted that within five years he would have the equivalent of an R-rated show on prime-time, network television. He achieved his goal in less than that time. In their conceit, such producers are neglecting the tastes and desires of a large percentage of the citizenry of the nation. Every survey made, every poll taken, shows a strong and substantial corps of people of high ideals, with faith in a Supreme Being, observing solid moral standards, and living with decency and integrity. And yet this segment of our society is seldom depicted by producers. (A notable exception is the CBS series *Touched by an Angel*, which television critics initially panned. Critics notwithstanding, this "feel-good" program that unabashedly touts the existence of God and communication with Him through heavenly beings has found an immense loyal audience.)

It is naïve to believe that a steady diet of blatant immorality, played out nightly in our living rooms, has no effect on people. I am always curious when individuals insist that what they watch on television or in movie theaters doesn't affect them. It was interesting to note that the going rate for a thirty-second advertising spot for the 1999 Super Bowl was 1.5 million dollars. Apparently, a host of advertisers felt confident that in thirty seconds' time they could influence their viewers to buy the products or services they were peddling. Are we really to believe that hours, leading to years, of television viewing will not affect attitudes about everything from family life to appropriate sexual relations?

Similarly, pornography, which is a seedbed for more blatant immorality, is no longer regarded as back-alley fare. In too many homes and lives, it is now regarded as a legitimate slice of entertainment. Pornography robs its victims of self-respect and of an appreciation of the beauties of life. It tears down those who indulge and pulls them into a slough of evil thoughts and possibly evil deeds. It seduces, destroys, and distorts the truth about love and intimacy. It is more deadly than a foul disease. Pornography is as addictive and self-destructive as illicit drugs, and it literally destroys the personal relationships of those who become its slaves.

Not one of us can afford to partake of this rubbish. We cannot risk the damage it does to the most precious of relationships—marriage—and to other interactions within the family. We cannot risk the effect it will have on our spirit and soul. Salacious videotapes, 900 telephone numbers, the filth found on the Internet, sensual magazines and movies—all are traps to be avoided like the deadliest of plagues.

Many years ago, I worked in a Denver railroad office, where I was in charge of the baggage and express traffic carried in passenger trains. One day I received a telephone call from my counterpart on another railroad in Newark, New Jersey, who said that a passenger train had arrived without its baggage car. Three hundred patrons were angry, as well they had a right to be.

We discovered that the train had been properly made up in Oakland, California, and had subsequently traveled, intact, to Salt Lake City, then to Denver, and on to St. Louis, from which station it was to depart to its destination on the east coast. But in the St. Louis railroad yard, a switchman had mistakenly moved a piece of steel just three inches. That piece of steel was a switch point, and the baggage car that should have been in Newark was in New Orleans, fourteen hundred miles away.

Prisons all over this country are filled with people who made unwise and even destructive choices, individuals who moved a switch point in their lives just a little and were soon on the wrong track going to the wrong place.

It is a matter of more than passing interest that the Lord, as he spoke to the multitude on the Mount, included this marvelous declaration: "Blessed are the pure in heart: for they shall see God" (Matthew 5:8). If only each of us would seek to be more pure! If only our society would place value on purity!

One popular professional athlete made headlines a few years ago when he suggested that with his high salary and superstar status came no obligation to be an "example" or "hero" to anyone, including the thousands of young people who admire him and wear jerseys adorned with his number because of his extraordinary athletic talent. How preposterous! How different might our society be if those who enjoyed the privilege of prominence and fame also felt the desire, if not the obligation, to celebrate virtue. Imagine the influence in this country of such high-profile endorsements of morality. Imagine the men and women, boys and girls, who would follow their examples! The impact would be staggering for the good.

I am old enough, and my childhood and youth occurred long enough ago, that I have had heroes to follow and great men to try to emulate throughout my life. My body of heroes grew to include such men as Washington, Jefferson, Lincoln, and other presidents of the United States. I was just sixteen when Charles Lindbergh flew across the Atlantic in the single-engine *Spirit of St. Louis,* landing thirty-three hours after departure. He became an instant larger-than-life hero to me. I can vividly recall newsboys running through the streets shouting "Extra! Extra!" as they peddled special editions of the paper. Lindbergh's triumph was thrilling because he had taken on the impossible and succeeded.

When I was in junior high school, my father took me to a lecture by Admiral Richard E. Byrd, who had commanded an expedition to the South Pole. His success was tremendously significant. I listened with rapt attention to his enthralling words. He too became a hero.

Through the years, I have come to admire many others. I am a direct descendant of Stephen Hopkins, who was a passenger on the *Mayflower.* He and the rest of that courageous band of early immigrants set out on a calm sea, but before their journey's end they wallowed through the mountainous waves of equinoctial storms. Arriving in America in late November, they faced a long and difficult winter, with no provisions other than those brought aboard the ship. In two or three months, half of the company died. Nonetheless, despite the terrible ordeals through which they had come, when the *Mayflower* left for England the following spring, not one of them returned with it. These heroes and heroines were men and women of tremendous physical and moral courage.

I feel sorry for today's generation, which seems bereft of heroes. Men and women who by virtue of their contributions and achievements seem larger than life, and who can be admired for the full breadth and depth of their moral makeup, are a vanishing breed.

On the other hand, I am satisfied that there are millions of good people in America and in other lands. Many married couples are faithful to each other. Their children are being reared in sobriety, industry, and faith in God. Given the strength of these families, I believe that the situation is far from hopeless. I am satisfied that there is no need to stand still and let the filth and violence overwhelm us, or to run in despair. The tide, high and menacing as it is, can be turned back if enough of the good people I have mentioned add their strength to the strength of the few who are now effectively working. The challenge to recognize evil and oppose it is one that every moral, virtuous person must accept.

It all begins with our own personal virtue. Reformation of the world begins with reformation of self. We cannot hope to influence others in the direction of moral virtue unless we live lives of virtue. The example of our virtuous living will carry a greater influence than will all the preaching, postulating, and theorizing in which we might indulge. We cannot expect to lift others unless we are standing on higher ground.

Respect for self is the beginning of cultivating virtue in men and women.

We live in an age of sloppy dress, sloppy manners, and regrettably, sloppy morals. For some unexplained reason, the false notion that sexual morality is unreasonably hard—too hard for the men and women of today to be expected to adhere to—is promoted almost constantly. The irony of the alternative is apparently lost on its advocates. The unbridled behavior leading to immorality is actually a harder choice than is the restraint required by sexual purity. Infidelity, promiscuity, and sexual indulgence, in all their forms, come trailing a host of ills: life-threatening disease; the insecurity of sexual involvement without commitment, or even without love, in many cases; the deterioration of one's feelings of value and self-worth; the breach of personal integrity; the threat of unwanted pregnancy, and so on. Morality requires discipline, yes. But is a little personal restraint more difficult than any of the aforementioned consequences? No clear-thinking person would insist that it is.

There also constantly appears the false rationalization that, long ago, virtue was easy, and only *now*, in this modern age, has it become difficult. Because self-control poses an element of challenge, it is said that we should, in a society that touts "freedom," accept moral breaches as "human" and therefore excusable and understandable. And yet, the proposal made by Potiphar's wife to Joseph in Egypt is not essentially different from that faced by men and women in our day. The major difference is that we are inundated with a blatant portrayal and even a celebration of immorality in nearly every form of communication and entertainment, and there appear to be more people who openly and vocally condone various kinds of immorality as issues of personal choice. What was labeled as indecent and immoral a few years ago is widely tolerated and even embraced today.

Yet each of us has a conscience. We know the difference between right and wrong. We do not have to be instructed concerning what is good and what is evil. We know when we have done the wrong thing, and we suffer pangs of conscience. We know when we have done the right thing, which results in a sense of inner peace and happiness.

Our challenge is to lift our thoughts above the filth, to discipline our acts into an example of virtue, to control our words so that we speak only that which is uplifting and leads to growth. These are the steps toward personal purity and virtue, the steps we must take in order to lift and invite others to a higher level of living.

These steps are achievable for all of us. The course of our lives is seldom determined by great, life-altering decisions. Our direction is more often set by the small, day-to-day choices that chart the track on which we run. This is the substance of our lives—making choices.

The lesson of the switch point is similar to the workings of a large and heavy farm gate. Such a gate moves very little at the hinges but a long way out at the circumference. A very small movement at the hinge brings long movement at the end of the gate.

So it is with our lives. A careless giving-in to an impulse, a poor decision, a momentary breach of self-discipline can wreak havoc, with consequences reaching farther than we could ever have imagined.

On a trip to Switzerland some years ago, I bought a package of edelweiss seeds. The seeds are like small, dry flecks of pepper, very tiny. But on the face of the package is pictured the mature plant, the flower that grows high in the Swiss Alps. Edelweiss weathers the storms raging through those mountains, blooms beneath the snow, and gives beauty to

Alpine slopes and meadows. They don't look like much, but the tiny seeds have within them the potential for vigorous and beautiful life.

So it is with each of us. Within us lies an incalculable potential for good. But the decisions we make determine the course of our lives and the makeup of our character. They determine whether we will live virtuously.

The churches of the world can help. Pope John Paul II's repeated warnings against moral pitfalls are impressive and wise. The Baptists have launched an important and earnest campaign for chastity. Many good people representing many faiths are standing strong against the wiles of the world.

That man or woman who knows and *believes* that he or she is a child of God, created by a Divine Father and gifted with a potential for the exercise of great and godlike virtues, will discipline himself or herself against the sordid, lascivious elements to which we are frequently and readily exposed.

When I was a boy growing up in Salt Lake City, most homes were heated with coal stoves. As a result, black smoke belched forth from almost every chimney. As winter came to a close, black soot and grime were everywhere, both inside and outside of the house. There was a ritual through which we passed each year—not a pleasant one, as we viewed it. It involved every member of the family and was known as "spring cleaning." When the weather warmed after the long winter, a week or so was designated as cleanup time, and Mother ran the show. All of the curtains were taken down, laundered, and carefully ironed. The windows were washed inside and out, and oh, what a job that was in our big, two-story house! Wallpaper was on all of the walls, and Father would bring home cans of wallpaper cleaner that looked like pink bread dough and had a pleasant, refreshing smell. We all pitched in. We would knead some of the cleaning dough in our hands, climb a ladder, and begin on the high ceiling, and then work down the walls. The dough was soon black from the dirt it lifted from the paper. It was a terrible, tiring task, but the results were like magic. When we stood back to compare the dirty surface with the clean, it was amazing to see how much better the clean walls looked, and to notice how dirty the walls had become without our realizing it.

We took up all of the carpets and dragged them to the backyard, where they were hung over the clothesline, one by one. Each of us boys would have a carpet beater, a device made of light steel rods with a wooden handle. As we beat the carpet, the dust would fly, and we would keep going until there was no dust left. We detested that work, but when all of it was done and everything was back in place, the result was wonderful. The house was clean; our spirits were renewed. The whole world looked better.

Spring cleaning, metaphorically speaking, is exactly what some of us need to do with our lives. Isaiah said: "Wash you, make you clean; put away the evil of your doings from before mine eyes; cease to do evil. . . . Come now, and let us reason together, saith the Lord: though your sins be as scarlet, they shall be as white as snow; though they be red like crimson, they shall be as wool" (Isaiah 1:16–18).

Though this suggestion may seem simple, it is also critical: Can we not turn our backs on immorality? Is it not possible for us as people to shun it? This is, of course, easier said than done. But each time we step closer toward a completely moral life, it will be so much easier the next time. What a wonderful thing it is for those who can say, "I am clean."

Both experience and divine wisdom dictate that moral virtue and cleanliness pave the way that leads to strength of character, peace of mind and heart, and happiness in life. There is no question that the way of safety and the road to a sense of genuine fulfillment lie in sexual abstinence before marriage and fidelity following marriage.

It has been my privilege on various occasions to converse with five presidents of the United States. At the conclusion of each such occasion, I have reflected on the rewarding experience of standing with confidence in the presence of the acknowledged leader of the free world. And then I have thought, what a wonderful thing, what a marvelous thing it would be to stand with confidence—unafraid and unashamed and unembarrassed—in the presence of God. This is the promise held out to every virtuous man and woman.

Some of us are fearful of what our peers will say if we adopt such a position. We might be looked on with disdain and criticized if we stand for what is right and promote a moral standard higher than that found among the masses. But the kingdom of God is not a democracy. Wickedness and righteousness are not legislated by majority vote. Right and wrong are not determined by polls or pundits, though many would have us believe otherwise. Evil never was happiness. Happiness lies in the power and the love and the sweet simplicity of virtue.

This is not to suggest that we be prudish. We need not slink off in a corner, as it were. We need not be ashamed. But if we were called upon to stand openly and give an accounting of ourselves, could we do it without embarrassment? If all the world were privy to our private behavior, would we feel confident and comfortable about the choices we have made? More importantly, are we at peace with ourselves?

Paul counseled Timothy, "Keep thyself pure" (1 Timothy 5:22). Those are simple words. But they are ever so important. Paul is saying, in effect: Stay away from those things that undermine and eventually destroy the soul. Stay away from that which leads to unclean thoughts, unclean language, and harmful behavior. Personal virtue is worth more than any salary, any bonus, any position or degree of prominence.

We must reverse the trend toward moral degeneration.

Is there a valid case for personal morality and virtue? It is the only way to freedom from regret. The peace of conscience that flows from personal virtue is the only personal peace that is not counterfeit. And beyond all of this is the unfailing promise of God to those who walk in virtue, "exceeding great and precious promises: that by these ye might be partakers of the divine nature" (2 Peter 1:4).

Channing Pollock once remarked: "A world in which everyone believed in the purity of women and the nobility of men, and acted accordingly, would be a very different world, but a grand place to live in." It would be a world of freedom in which the human spirit might grow to undreamed-of glory, and a world of peace—the peace of clear conscience, of unsullied love, of fidelity, of unfailing trust and loyalty. This may appear an unattainable dream for the world. But, for each of us individually, it can become a reality, and the world will become so much richer and stronger because of the virtue of *each individual life.*

A great moral reformation will occur only as reformation takes place in the hearts, minds, and lives of each of us; as morality is reinstated as a priority in the homes of the country; and as men and women, boys and girls, realize their lives are missing a critical moral component and determine to seek a life of virtue.

Four

Our Fading *Civility*

Civility carries with it the essence of courtesy, politeness, and consideration of others. All of the education and accomplishments in the world will not count for much unless they are accompanied by marks of gentility, of respect for others, of going the extra mile.

One day, when I was about five years of age, several friends and I were seated on the front porch of my home when an African American family walked down the street. I made some kind of disparaging remark. I do not remember what I said, and I do not know that they heard me. But my mother, who was just inside the house, did hear me. She called me and my friends inside and immediately proceeded to sit us down and deliver a lecture I can still remember. She gave us to understand, in no uncertain terms, that among the peoples of the earth there is neither inferiority nor superiority; that we are all sons and daughters of God and therefore sisters and brothers with each other; and that we have an obligation to respect and help one another.

I have carried that simple lesson with me all my life. I learned many years later that my mother, at about age fourteen, had stood up for and befriended, in school, an African American boy who had been taunted by others. I learned this from the individual himself. He had grown to manhood and was serving as sergeant-at-arms in the state legislature.

In the course of my life, I have mingled widely with people of all races and cultures, all levels of income and education, and all stations. Particularly in this day of sophisticated communication, the world is our neighborhood, and its peoples, regardless of status, are our friends and neighbors. I include all within the compass of the mandate of the Savior, who said, "Thou shalt love the Lord thy God with all thy heart, and with all thy soul, and with all thy mind. This is the first and great commandment. And the second is like unto it, Thou shalt love thy neighbour as thyself" (Matthew 22:37–39).

We have reason to be deeply concerned that around the world, including in America, there still exists much prejudice—a tendency to separate ourselves according to our differences rather than to rejoice in the diversity and richness of texture those differences provide. We may feel some optimism, however, that interracial dialogue is gradually getting better. In a greater number of countries, there is more tolerance, more respect, more acknowledgment of the good in each of us. The fight has been uphill, but it is being won.

On a recent trip to Africa, I met tens of thousands of the good men and women of that continent. When they are given opportunity, they respond. They are kind and generous. They are intelligent and have a wonderful capacity to do things. They are good. They are beautiful. I have had much the same reaction among the peoples of Asia and Latin America, in the islands of the South Pacific, and throughout eastern and western Europe.

Differences of race and culture are obvious, as are distinctions among various religious and other persuasions. I fear, however, that far too often we make too much of our differences. We therefore obscure and at times completely overlook the significant and enduring ways in which we are alike. We have cultural and theological differences, but I believe we are of one mind in our awareness of the evils and problems of the world. I believe we all recognize our great responsibility and opportunity to stand united for those qualities in public and private life that speak of virtue and morality. I believe we agree on the need for respect for all men and women as children of God, the need for civility and courtesy in our relationships, and the need to preserve the family as the most fundamental and important unit of society.

Most of us carry in our hearts a desire to assist the poor, to lift the distressed, to give comfort, hope, and help to all who are in trouble and pain. We recognize the need to heal the wounds of society and replace with optimism and faith the pessimism of our times. There is no need for recrimination or criticism against one another.

An article of the faith to which I subscribe states: "We claim the privilege of worshiping Almighty God according to the dictates of our own conscience, and allow all men the same privilege; let them worship how, where, or what they may." I hope to find myself always on the side of those defending this position. Our strength lies in our freedom to choose. There is strength even in our diversity. But there is greater strength in the God-given mandate to each of us to work for the uplifting and blessing of all His sons and daughters, regardless of their ethnic or national origin or other differences.

We are sons and daughters of God, each a member of the divine family. As surely as He is our father, we are all brothers and sisters. We simply must work unitedly to remove from our hearts and to drive from our society all elements of hatred, bigotry, racism, and other divisive actions and words that limit a person's ability to progress, learn, and be fully accepted. Snide remarks or racial slurs, hateful epithets, malicious gossip, and mean and vicious rumormongering have no place among us.

Each of us is human, subject to the problems that afflict humans. We should not tolerate laziness, dishonesty, or betrayal. But neither should we condemn others for such apparent lapses. Instead, we can reach out to help them carry the burdens of sickness and financial difficulty, and even the weaknesses and shortcomings with which they are grappling. None of us needs someone who only points out our areas of weakness and the ways in which we have fallen short. We need someone who encourages us to go forward, to try again, to reach a little higher this time. Excellence is difficult to achieve in a vacuum.

Said Paul to the Romans, "We then that are strong ought to bear the infirmities of the weak." And then he added these significant words, "and not to please ourselves" (Romans 15:1). We have an obligation to assist one another, to build one another. No one of us is perfect; we have all made mistakes. Each of us occasionally needs to be disciplined and instructed. But such feedback ought to be offered in a spirit of correcting, helping, and strengthening. Can we not support each other? Teach one another? And encourage and praise those with whom we come in contact?

Imagine how our own families, let alone the world, would change if we vowed to keep faith with one another, strengthen one another, look for and accentuate the virtues in one another, and speak graciously concerning one another. Imagine the cumulative effect if we treated each other with respect and acceptance, if we willingly provided support. Such interactions practiced on a small scale would surely have a rippling effect throughout our homes and communities and, eventually, society at large.

Throughout the march of history, society has made progress when people have lived together in communities, with respect and concern for one another. These virtues are the hallmark of civilization. And yet, at times, we must pause to question how much progress we have really made. The century that has now drawn to a close has witnessed more death and suffering from war than any other era in human history. Even today, we witness the tragedies occurring in Liberia; in Israel and its neighbors; in Bosnia, Albania, and Serbia; in Ireland; in Iraq; and in many other regions around the world. Civility and mutual respect are unknown among people who are reared to hate and despise others.

Much closer to home, civility appears to be fading. Witness the recent growth of gangs in this country. Their members show no respect for their enemies and little respect for life. They mar beautiful walls and buildings with ugly graffiti, and they evidently think only in terms of self. Crime is essentially an absence of civility. A study sponsored by the National

Institute of Justice concluded that crime costs Americans at least 450 billion dollars a year. It is difficult to comprehend a figure of such magnitude. The Defense Department's budget in 1995 was 252 billion dollars, so the cost of crime is essentially twice the amount we spend to defend our nation.

It is appalling. It is alarming. And when all is said and done, the cost can be attributed almost entirely to human greed, to uncontrolled passion, to a total disregard for the rights of others—in other words, to a lack of civility. As one writer has said, "People might think of a civilized community as one in which there is a refined culture. Not necessarily; first and foremost it is one in which the mass of people subdue their selfish instincts in favor of the common well-being."

This writer continued: "In recent years the media have raised boorishness to an art form. The hip heroes of movies today deliver gratuitous put-downs to ridicule and belittle anyone who gets in their way. Bad manners, apparently, make a saleable commodity. Television situation comedies wallow in vulgarity, stand-up comedians base their acts on insults to their audiences, and talk show hosts become rich and famous by snarling at callers and heckling guests."

All of this speaks of anything but refinement. It speaks of anything but courtesy. It speaks of anything but civility and tolerance. Rather, it speaks of rudeness and crudeness and an utter insensitivity to the feelings and rights of others.

It is so with much of the language of the day. In schools and in the workplace, evil, filthy, coarse language is common. It too marks a lack of civility. The finger of the Lord wrote on the tablets of stone, "Thou shalt not take the name of the Lord thy God in vain; for the Lord will not hold him guiltless that taketh his name in vain" (Exodus 20:7).

Those who routinely take the name of God in vain and resort to filthy, crude language only advertise the poverty of their vocabularies, a glaring paucity in their powers of expression, and a flaw in their moral makeup. Civility invites the ability to speak, to converse, to communicate effectively. It is a tremendous asset, both personally and professionally. There are few things more delightful than participating in a conversation with bright and happy people who have something to say, whose dialogue is witty, scintillating, and punctuated not only by good humor but by thoughtful dialogue about serious and important topics. It is never necessary in such conversation—indeed, it would be offensive—to profane the name of Deity or to use salty and salacious language of any kind. There is plenty of humor in the world without resorting to dirty jokes or uncouth language.

I will never forget coming home from school one day as a first-grader. I threw my books on the table and took the name of the Lord in vain, expressing my relief that school was out for the day. Mother heard me and was horrified. Without uttering a word, she took me by the hand and led me to the bathroom, pulled out a clean washcloth and a bar of soap, told me to open my mouth, and proceeded to wash my mouth with that terrible soap. I blubbered and protested. She stayed at it for what seemed a long time, and then said, "Don't let me ever hear such words from your lips again."

The taste was terrible. The reprimand was worse. I have never forgotten it. How can one profane the name of God and then kneel before Him in prayer? Profanity separates us from Him who has supreme power to help us. Profanity wounds the spirit and demeans the soul.

Sloppy language and sloppy ways go together. Those who are truly educated have learned more than the sciences, the humanities, law, engineering, and the arts. They carry with them a certain polish that marks them as loving the better qualities of life, the culture that adds luster to the mundane world of which they are a part, a patina that puts a quiet glow on what otherwise might be base metal.

Said the Savior to the multitude: "Ye are the salt of the earth: but if the salt have lost its savour, wherewith shall it be salted? it is thenceforth good for nothing, but to be cast out, and to be trodden under foot of men" (Matthew 5:13).

Civility, I submit, is what gives savor to our lives. It is the salt that speaks of good taste, good manners, good breeding. It becomes an expression of the Golden Rule: "Therefore all things whatsoever ye would that men should do to you, do ye even so to them" (Matthew 7:12).

Civility covers a host of matters in how one human being relates to another with basic human kindness and goodness. Civility requires us to restrain and control ourselves, and at the same time to act with respect toward others.

George Washington, who was known early in his life for his hot temper, began the process of subduing his passions by copying into a personal notebook a translated version of a French book of etiquette that dated to the sixteenth century. This book contained 110 rules or measures of civility, which included such standards as the following:

Every action in company ought to be with some sign of respect to those present.

Show not yourself glad at the misfortune of another, though he were your enemy.

Undertake not to teach your equal in the art he himself professes; it savors of arrogancy.

Mock not nor jest at anything of importance; break no jests that are sharp or biting; and if you deliver anything witty or pleasant, abstain from laughing therat yourself.

Use no reproachful language against anyone, neither curses nor revilings.

Civility is the root of the word *civilization*. It carries with it the essence of courtesy, politeness, and consideration of others. How very much of it we have lost in our contemporary society! All of the education and accomplishments in the world will not count for much unless they are accompanied by marks of gentility, of respect for others, of going the extra mile, of serving as a good Samaritan, of being men and women who look beyond our own selfish interests to the good of others. Only as we do so will we find fulfillment. In some respects, it truly is a "jungle out there." The absence of civility creates the jungle. No matter the extent of our education, no matter our achievements in science, business, the professions, or whatever—if that other dimension of which I have spoken is missing, we will lack that which is most precious. We will be deficient in the godly quality of reaching out with respect and kindness, with courtesy and appreciation and maturity, toward our fellow travelers here on planet earth.

I am not suggesting that we be soft and docile. I admire enthusiasm and even assertion in the pursuit of worthy objectives. But I also hope that we will be enthusiastic and aggressive in reaching out to lift, to help, to encourage those whose lives we can touch in good ways.

I rented a house once to a graduate student from the Midwest who was working on a doctorate in physics under a celebrated professor at the University of Utah. This student said to me about his graduate adviser, "He is the most remarkable teacher I have ever known. He has a sense of charity coupled with an expectation of excellence. He will not let a student fail.

"When he has a student who is having a difficult time, he assigns an A-grade student to work with him. The result is that the one who was stumbling comes to understanding and proficiency. And the one who serves without fee as tutor gains a better knowledge of the subject and develops a wonderful sense of service and kindness toward others."

This is the essence of civility—to extend, without price, a helping or lifting hand to those in need; to anxiously look for ways to strengthen those who may have less than we do.

What a truly remarkable and exciting time is this era in which we live. There have been more scientific discoveries during my lifetime than during all previous centuries of the history of the world. Most of the great discoveries of medicine have occurred during this time. Polio, once the summer dread of every mother, is almost entirely gone. It is hard to believe. The miracle drugs that have saved the lives of millions; open-heart surgery; organ transplants—these and many other similar procedures have become commonplace. Even the complex door of cancer cures appears to be opening a crack.

Like the "man on the flying trapeze," we fly through the air to the great cities and even to the obscure and isolated outbacks of the world with the greatest of ease. Computers have changed our lives. The atom has been harnessed, for good or ill. The creations of science are endless and almost too great to even dream of. They make it easier for us to attend to our own needs and to help each other.

With such resources and advantages accessible, my hope is that we will look beyond our own immediate needs and lives, and find ways to make great and significant contributions to our society. For, despite all of the wonders of this age, we have the same old social problems that we had generations ago. There is still so much poverty and stark want across the world, so much rebellion and meanness, so much sleaze and filth, so many broken homes and destroyed families, so many lonely people living colorless lives without hope, so much distress everywhere.

Shakespeare's Romeo declares, "He jests at scars that never felt a wound." There are thousands out there who nurse wounds and carry scars from the buffetings of life. For this reason, I make a plea that with all of our *getting*, we will also *give* to make the world a little better.

Many individuals around the globe are setting magnificent examples of the difference even one person can make when that person is devoted to improving the well-being of others. In the Philippines, an able American doctor, in his spare time, gathered Filipino doctors around him and taught them the restorative surgery that takes away the cleft palates and the facial disfigurements of many children. Lives have been dramatically and wonderfully changed as those newly handsome and beautiful boys and girls have emerged from the operating room. This doctor has now greatly enlarged his efforts and involved many others in a number of countries.

I was in the Dallas airport one day, waiting for a plane, when a man walked up to me and introduced himself. He was a medical doctor on his way to Central America. Every year, he goes there for a month to perform, without fee, numerous operations to help those who would be utterly helpless without the kind of assistance he can give.

Truly great men and women resolve to dedicate a part of their lives and time to those in distress. Helping hands can lift someone out of the mire of difficulty. Steady voices can provide encouragement for some who might otherwise simply give up. Skills can change, in a remarkable and wonderful way, the lives of those in need. It is not enough for any of us to get a job and feverishly work to produce income that leads only to personal comfort. We may gain some recompense in all of this, but we will not gain the ultimate satisfaction. When we serve others, we best serve our God.

Generally speaking, the most miserable people I know are those who are obsessed with themselves. By and large, if we complain about life, it is because we are thinking only of ourselves. For many years, there was a sign on the wall of a shoe shop I patronized that read: "I complained because I had no shoes until I saw a man who had no feet." The most effective medicine for the sickness of self-pity is to lose ourselves in the service of others.

The best antidote I know for worry is work. The best cure for weariness is the challenge of helping someone who is even more tired. One of the great ironies of life is this: He or she who serves almost always benefits more than he or she who is served.

Strong hands and determined wills can improve the world and the condition of its people. I have a friend, a very successful attorney in Seattle, whose wife said to him not long after their marriage, "Let's give a quarter of our time, for the rest of our lives, to the improvement of the world and the blessing of its people." They have kept that promise. His wife has died, but my friend continues to be recognized for the wonders he has done for the Northwest. His leadership has attracted others to work with him to clean up the waters of the Seattle area, to preserve the great forests of the Northwest, to build a beautiful new civic center that is constructed over a freeway and utilizes the air rights above it. He is now growing old. He will not be remembered for the cases he argued brilliantly in the courts of law. He will be remembered for the great projects and the humanitarian aid he undertook and carried through to fulfillment for his community and its people.

On a trip to the Philippines, I met a couple whom I had not seen in years. The weather was steamy hot, as it always is in Bacolod, the center of the once-thriving Filipino sugar industry. But there were my friend and his wife. When I asked them what they were doing there, they replied that they had come to help the people. When I inquired about their living conditions, they responded that they lived in a little house on one of the many islands of the Philippines. I couldn't help thinking about the last time I had seen them. They were living in a beautiful home in Scarsdale, New York. He was a widely recognized and honored chemist who worked for one of the multinational companies headquartered in New York. He had been credited with discovering the chemical ingredients of a product now sold around the world. He was well paid and highly respected. But he and his wife had retired, sold their estate, given their children what furniture they wanted and donated the rest to others, and made themselves available to serve among the less fortunate. They had come to the Philippines to heal the suffering people, to give encouragement and strength, hope and faith. They were there to heal wounds of contention and to care for those with diseased bodies and frustrated minds. They were living humbly among the poor, down at the level of the people, but standing straight and tall to lift with strong hands.

I learned a great lesson that day, watching my good friends as they moved among a people they had grown to love. In the long run, it will not be enough for anyone who desires a sense of fulfillment and purpose to be an able lawyer, a practitioner of medicine, a skilled architect, a proficient engineer, or whatever. We need another dimension in our lives, a compelling need and drive within each of us to feel that somehow, somewhere we have made a difference—that our lives have mattered.

It is not enough just to be good. We must be good for something. We must contribute good to the world. The world must be a better place for our presence. And the good that is in us must be spread to others. This is the measure of our civility.

I don't suppose that many of us will be remembered a thousand years from now. But in this world so filled with problems, so constantly threatened by dark and evil challenges, we can and must rise above mediocrity, above indifference. We can become involved and speak with a strong voice for that which is right and good, and we can lend our efforts and our resources to helping those who have been saddled with handicaps and burdens.

Wendell Phillips once made this significant observation: "How prudently most men creep into nameless graves, while now and then one or two forget themselves into immortality!"

James Russell Lowell, in *The Vision of Sir Launfal,* wrote:

> Who gives himself with his alms feeds three,—
> Himself, his hungering neighbor, and Me.

Caring for others, seeing and reaching beyond our own wants and comforts, cultivating kindness and gentility toward others from all of life's situations and circumstances—these are of the essence of civility, a virtue to be admired, a virtue to be acquired.

Learning: "With All Thy Getting Get Understanding"

No matter how old we become, we can acquire knowledge and use it. We can gather wisdom and profit from it. We can grow and progress and improve—and, in the process, strengthen the lives of those within our circle of influence.

I love to learn. I relish any opportunity to acquire knowledge. Indeed, I believe in and have vigorously supported, throughout my life, the pursuit of education—for myself and for others. I was able to obtain a university education during the Great Depression, and from that time forward I have never been satiated with the pursuit of knowledge. From my point of view, learning is both a practical matter and a spiritual one.

Reduced to its simplest definition, education is the training of the mind and the body. Education is the great conversion process under which abstract knowledge becomes useful and productive activity. It is something that need never stop. No matter how old we become, we can acquire knowledge and use it. We can gather wisdom and profit from it. We can grow and progress and improve—and, in the process, strengthen the lives of those within our circle of influence. We can enrich our lives dramatically through the miracle of reading and exposure to the arts. The older I grow, the more I enjoy the words of thoughtful writers, ancient and modern. I savor that which they have learned and processed and recorded for others to read.

I believe that the glory of God is intelligence, and that the Almighty takes delight in our efforts to improve and enrich and enhance our minds. We live in a world where knowledge is expanding at an ever accelerating rate. We must learn to drink deeply from this phenomenal reservoir of wisdom and human experience. May I be so bold as to suggest that far too many people spend far too much time mesmerized by the mindless drivel that too often inhabits television airwaves, videos, and other forms of electronic media. What a contrast it is, a refreshing and liberating contrast, to read the great literature of the ages, or the word of God as recorded in sacred books of scripture.

I have in my home library a set of the Harvard Classics that originally belonged to my father. Though he was not a man of great financial means, he was an educated and thoughtful man who placed a high priority on language and learning. I still refer to this fifty-volume set of books, just as I did more than sixty years ago as a university student. It is a treasury of timeless literature, an encyclopedic presentation of the great thoughts of men and women who, in their eras, struggled with serious problems, thought deeply, prayed mightily, and expressed themselves in ways both challenging and beautiful.

In our home also was a room we called the library. It had a solid table and a good lamp, three or four comfortable chairs with good light, and hundreds of books in cases that lined the walls. We were never forced to read, but the books were placed where they were handy and where we could get at them whenever we wished. There were also magazines, books on technical subjects, dictionaries, scriptures, and atlases. There was quiet in that room. It was understood that it was a place to read and study and write, to ponder and meditate.

There was no television, of course, at that time. Radio came along while I was growing up. But my parents created within our home an environment of learning, and they made it clear—more by their actions and priorities than by anything they said—that they valued learning. I grew up believing that it was desirable to be informed, to be educated, to increase one's understanding about the world and its peoples. I would not have anyone believe that we were scholars, for we were not. But we were exposed to great literature, to great ideas from great thinkers.

At that early age, perhaps without realizing it at the time, I came to believe that we must never stop learning. The more we learn, the more we are in a position to learn. I urge parents everywhere to make a determined effort to create and cultivate within their homes an atmosphere of learning and the growth that will come of it.

Children who are exposed to books at early ages have scholastic advantages throughout their lives. Parents who fail to read to their small children do a disservice to them as well as to themselves. It takes time, yes, much of it. It takes self-discipline and planning. It takes organizing and budgeting the minutes and hours of the day. But it is never boring to watch young minds come to know characters, expressions, and ideas. Good reading can become a love affair, far more fruitful in long-term effects than many other activities to which children give their time. It has been estimated that the average child in the United States watches something approaching 8,000 hours of television before he or she even begins school. What a difference might it make, what an influence could it have in the homes of this country if parents were to work at creating an atmosphere of learning and education at home, so that children were exposed at an early age to thoughts and concepts and attitudes that would build and motivate them for good throughout their lives.

Said Solomon, "With all thy getting get understanding" (Proverbs 4:7). Within good libraries we have available the wisdom, the knowledge, the learning of all the generations who have gone before us. Never before has the dissemination of information been accomplished with such fluidity and ease. The Internet has opened a vast reservoir of information to almost anyone who owns a computer.

A man who is driven by much pressure because of the demands of his various responsibilities said to me not long ago, "Oh, if only I had time to read a good book, and a book of my choosing!" Surely all of us can find a way to incorporate into our daily lives a regular pattern of study, a regular opportunity to grow and absorb and learn from the great writers of the world. I am not suggesting that we must become geniuses. Most of us will never fall within that designation. But I have concluded that the work of the world is done by basically ordinary people who have learned to work in an extraordinary way. It is done by those who have had the good sense to learn from those who have gone before them. One does not have to be a genius to get ahead. One does not have to be brilliant to make a difference in this world, to reach out and help and serve and lead others. Such service, such inspiration, and such devoted leadership often come from those who are well versed in the history of the world, and who therefore have a personal database of information from which they can draw.

The learning process is endless. We must read, we must observe, we must assimilate, and we must ponder that to which we expose our minds. I believe in the evolution of the mind, the heart, and the soul of humanity. I believe in improvement. I believe in growth. There is nothing quite as invigorating as being able to evaluate and then solve a difficult problem, to grapple with something that seems almost unsolvable and then find a resolution.

For such reasons, and because the pace and complexity of life demand it, we cannot afford to stop learning and growing and progressing. We must not rest in our personal development—development that is emotional and spiritual as well as mental. There is so much to learn and so little time in which to learn it. I confess that I am constantly appalled by the scarcity of my knowledge, and the one resentment I carry concerns the many pressing demands that limit the opportunity for reading. Nonetheless, each of us, whether we are thirty or ninety, can keep growing. Each of us, regardless of our constraints or circumstances, can find a way to study and grow. Our industry in so doing will cause the years to pass faster than we might wish, but they will be filled with a sweet and wonderful zest that will add flavor to life and power to our personal influence and ability to teach and lead.

Many events that take place around us provide constant reminders that there is cause for alarm in our nation. It is shocking to read, for instance, that illiteracy is on the rise. It is almost unthinkable that, in such an abundant society, many adults cannot read. A story in the *New York Times* published under the headline "Study Says Half of Adults in U.S. Lack Reading and Math Abilities" offered some sobering statistics based on a study of more than 26,000 Americans above age fifteen:

> Nearly half of the nation's 191 million adult citizens are not proficient enough in English to write a letter about a billing error or to calculate the length of a bus trip from a published schedule, according to a four-year Federal study. The study, released yesterday by the Education Department, presented a bleak statistical portrait of the nation's literacy. . . . Businesses estimate they lose $25 billion to $30 billion a year nationwide in lost productivity, errors and accidents attributable to poor literacy.

One of the reasons for this condition lies in the manner in which so many people—and particularly so many youth and young adults—spend much of their time. I deplore the waste of the intellectual resources of so many people in this nation.

A former editor of the *Chicago Tribune* wrote:

> What is the mystery . . . about a society that has the manners of a rock band, the morals of a soap opera, the decision-making ability of the Simpsons and wants to pay

for government with Visa and American Express? Why should we be surprised that our underlying culture is constructed from the ratings-based, give-them-what-they-want, remote-controlled, quick-zap world of commercial television?

C. S. Lewis wrote:

We have lived to see the second death of ancient learning. In our time something which was once the possession of all educated men has shrunk to being the technical accomplishment of a few specialists. . . . If one were looking for a man who could not read Virgil though his father could, he might be found more easily in the twentieth century than in the fifth.

Our world needs straightening up. It needs leadership. It needs enlightenment. It needs those who are able to analyze problems and suggest solutions, those who can draw upon the past to make intelligent decisions for the future, those who understand the ramifications of certain kinds of actions, those who appreciate fully the interplay between virtue and morality and integrity and the fabric of society. Georg Wilhelm Friedrich Hegel once made a statement to the effect that those who do not read history will have to repeat it. How sobering a thought! As unthinkable as it might have been to imagine that the atrocities of Hitler's Germany could ever be repeated, we have witnessed in today's world the attempts at "ethnic cleansing."

None of us can assume that we have learned enough. I have lived long enough now to say with certainty that as the door closes on one phase of life, it opens on another. It therefore behooves us, and is our charge, to grow constantly toward eternity in what must be a ceaseless quest for truth. And as we search for truth, let us look for the good, the beautiful, and the positive.

I looked the other day with wonder, and even some affection, at a 1916 Model T Ford. It brought back a thousand memories of my childhood, for a vehicle like this was the first automobile we ever owned in our family. It was a thing of complete wonder when we were children. Today's generation knows almost nothing of these cars. They are seen only in the Smithsonian and in history books. They had no battery; the source of electricity was a magneto. At night, the intensity of the headlights depended on the speed of the motor. If the motor were kept running at high speed, the lights were bright. If the motor slowed down, the lights became a sickly yellow.

It is so with our minds. If we keep them sharpened on good literature and uplifting entertainment, if we are constantly interested in learning new things and acquiring new skills, personal development is inevitable and the light of our personality and our character shines ever brighter. If we starve them with the drivel of miserable shows and cheap and shoddy literature, they become poor indeed.

Dr. Joshua Liebman once observed:

[T]he great thing is that as long as we live we have the privilege of growing. We can learn new skills, engage in new kinds of work, devote ourselves to new causes, make new friends. Accepting then the truth that we are capable in some directions and limited in others, that genius is rare, that mediocrity is the portion of most of us, let us remember that we can and must change ourselves. Until the day of our death we can grow. We can tap hidden resources in our makeup.

We live in a world that has tremendous advantages. We benefit from marvelous advances made in such short periods of time that we are routinely in danger of taking for granted the comforts that surround us. For example, it is a simple thing for us to drive from point A to point B. But consider for a moment the complex processes involved in the development, manufacture, and sale of our automobile; the design and building of the highway we choose to follow; the availability of the fuel, which was refined from oil that was in all likelihood lifted from the depths of the earth in some distant place; and the thousand other details behind a simple drive from one location to another. Think for a moment about the tremendous technology behind the fabric of our clothing, the paper on which we write, the homes in which we live, the computers that now connect us electronically and immediately to the rest of the world. These and myriad other things that make our lives possible and comfortable are based on information, on knowledge, on learning. Education is the backbone of our society, of the world of commerce and finance, of medicine and law and architecture, of music and art.

Some years ago, I stood at the bedside of a friend, a strong and handsome man who had fallen victim to polio. Unable to breathe with his own strength, he lay in a great iron lung, which noisily and mechanically breathed for him. But despite all the efforts in his behalf, his body wasted, and while his beloved wife and children watched him struggle, he grew weaker and eventually died. His grandchildren, whom I also know, are now saved from so terrifying an illness and death by a drop of vaccine. That giant step for the conquest of disease, and others of similar value, came of knowledge and information, and of their inspired application.

I remember a scientist, a celebrated chemist, who spoke on the challenge of learning continuously. He said that on the day he received his PhD in chemistry, he thought he knew it all. But every year now, there is enough new literature published in his field to equal in bulk a complete edition of the *Encyclopedia Britannica*.

Never was there a more urgent need for vast quantities of information to keep the machinery of our society functioning and advancing. Brigham Young, after whom is named the largest church-owned university in the United States, said this about the application of such knowledge:

> There is no ingenious mind that has ever invented anything beneficial to the human family but what he obtained it from the one Source, whether he knows or believes it or not. There is only one Source whence men obtain wisdom, and that is God, the Fountain of all wisdom; and though men may claim to make their discoveries by their own wisdom, by meditation and reflection, they are indebted to our Father in heaven for all.

Each day, we are made increasingly aware of the fact that life is more than science and mathematics, more than history and literature. There is need for another education, without which the substance of our secular learning may lead only to our destruction. I refer to the education of the heart, of the conscience, of the character, of the spirit—those indefinable aspects of our personalities and characters that determine so certainly what we are and what we do in our relationships one with another. Let us not forget that "the fear of the Lord is the beginning of wisdom" (Proverbs 9:10), and that we are able to learn both by study and by faith in the Almighty. Indeed, the schooling of our spirits is as important as the schooling of our minds, if not more important.

The year 1979 marked the centennial anniversary of electric light. As profound as such light is, another light is known and available to each of us. If we cultivate it, it can become an even greater influence in our lives. The principle is this: That which comes from God is light, and the person who receives and invites this light into his or her life will receive more light. It is that simple. It is that profound.

In the Sermon on the Mount, the Savior proclaimed that a city on a hill cannot be hid. He then taught that people do not light a candle only to put it under a bushel. Instead, they place it on a candlestick, where it may give light to all present. Then he issued this profound challenge, one that has the power to literally change the world: "Let your light so shine before men, that they may see your good works, and glorify your Father which is in heaven" (Matthew 5:14–16).

It is not enough just to live, just to survive. It is incumbent on each of us to equip ourselves to do something worthwhile in society—to acquire more and more light, so that our personal light can help illuminate a darkened world. And this is made possible through learning, through educating ourselves, through progressing and growing in both mind and spirit.

The Twin Virtues of
Forgiveness and *Mercy*

Hatred always fails and bitterness always destroys. Are there virtues more in need of application in our day, a time marked by litigious proceedings and heated exchanges, than those of forgiving, forgetting, and extending mercy to those who may have wronged us or let us down?

We have much for which we should be grateful: the comforts of our modern society, sophisticated global communication that allows us easy access to the entire world, and the privilege of living in a free and prosperous land. It would become us, as a grateful people, to reach out with a spirit of forgiveness and mercy and an attitude of love and compassion toward all, particularly those we may feel have wronged us.

We have need of forgiveness, mercy, and compassion. The whole world has need of them, for they are of the essence of goodness. We need these qualities in homes where tiny molehills of misunderstanding grow into mountains of argument, and where parents and children sometimes hang on to an old grievance for years and even for a lifetime. We need them among neighbors whose insignificant differences lead to undying bitterness. We need them among business associates who quarrel and refuse to compromise or forgive when, in most instances, a willingness to sit down together, exercise compassion, and speak quietly one to another could resolve the matter to the blessing of all. Too often, too many people spend their days blaming others, nurturing grudges, and planning retribution.

Guy de Maupassant, the French writer, tells the story of a peasant named Hauchecome who came on market day to the village. While walking through the public square, his eye caught sight of a piece of string lying on the cobblestones. He picked it up and put it in his pocket. His actions were observed by the village harness maker, with whom he had previously had a dispute.

Later in the day, the loss of a purse was reported. Hauchecome was arrested on the accusation of the harness maker. He was taken before the mayor, to whom he protested his innocence, showing the piece of string that he had picked up. But he was not believed and was laughed at.

The next day, the purse was found and Hauchecome was absolved of any wrongdoing. But, resentful of the indignity he had suffered because of a false accusation, he became embittered and would not let the matter die. Unwilling to forgive and forget, he thought and talked of little else. He neglected his farm. Everywhere he went, everyone he met had to be told of the injustice. By day and by night he brooded over it. Obsessed with his grievance, he became desperately ill and died. In the delirium of his death struggles, he repeatedly murmured, "A piece of string, a piece of string."

With variations of characters and circumstances, that story is relived many times in our own day. How difficult it seems to be to forgive those who have injured us! We are prone to brood on the evil done us, and that brooding becomes as a gnawing and destructive canker. Are there virtues more in need of application in our day, a time marked by litigious proceedings and heated exchanges, than those of forgiving, forgetting, and extending mercy to those who may have wronged us or let us down?

There are those who would look upon these virtues as signs of weakness. But it takes neither strength nor intelligence to brood in anger over wrongs suffered, to go through life with a spirit of vindictiveness, to dissipate one's abilities in planning retribution, or to press a grievance when someone else is "down." There is no genius or peace in the nursing of a grudge. You've no doubt heard the clever phrase, often spoken in jest, "I don't get mad, I just get even." Though the statement invites a chuckle, there is nothing humorous about it, for it promotes a spirit of retaliation and one-upmanship rather than conciliation, cooperation, and friendship.

Paul speaks of "the weak and beggarly elements" of our lives (Galatians 4:9). Is there anything more weak or beggarly than the disposition to wear out one's life in an unending round of bitter thoughts and scheming gestures?

There is great wisdom and restraint in turning the other cheek and, in the process, trying to overcome evil with good. General Omar Bradley is quoted as having said: "We have grasped the mystery of the atom and rejected the Sermon on the Mount. . . . Ours is a world of nuclear giants and ethical infants. We know more about war than we know about peace, more about killing than we know about living."

One day, a feuding couple came to visit with me. There was bitterness between them. At one time, their love had been deep and true, but each had developed a habit of speaking of the faults of the other. Unwilling to forgive the kinds of mistakes we all make or to forget them and live above them with forbearance, they had carped at one another until the love they once knew had been smothered. It turned to ashes with the decree of a "no-fault" divorce, and now each of them has only loneliness and recrimination. I believe that had there been even a small measure of repentance and forgiveness, they would still be together, enjoying the companionship that had so richly blessed their earlier years.

Those who nurture in their hearts poisonous enmity toward another would be well served to ask the Almighty for strength to forgive and to extend the hand of mercy. Hatred always fails, and bitterness always destroys. Just an expression of the desire to forgive is of the very substance of repentance. It may not be easy, and it may not come quickly. But when it is sought with sincerity and cultivated, it *will* come. And even if the person who has been forgiven continues to pursue and threaten, the sincere effort toward effecting a reconciliation brings a peace that is otherwise unattainable. That peace will be the peace of Him who said: "For if ye forgive men their trespasses, your heavenly Father will also forgive you: But if you forgive not men their trespasses, neither will your Father forgive your trespasses" (Matthew 6:14–15).

We are all familiar with the injunction found in the Sermon on the Mount, "Love your enemies, bless them that curse you, do good to them that hate you, and pray for them which despitefully use you, and persecute you" (Matthew 5:43–44).

During the same sermon, the Lord included another similar injunction: "Ye have heard that it hath been said, An eye for an eye, and a tooth for a tooth: But I say unto you, That ye resist not evil: but whosoever shall smite thee on thy right cheek, turn to him the other also. . . . And whosoever shall compel thee to go a mile, go with him twain" (Matthew 5:38–41).

Frankly, most of us have not reached that stage of compassion and love and forgiveness. It is not easy to reach. It requires a self-discipline almost greater than we are capable of. It requires the ability to let go of our pride. The application of this principle of forgiveness, difficult to live but wondrous in its curative powers, would have a miraculous effect on our troubled homes. Selfishness is the cause of most of our misery. It is as a cankering disease. The healing power of Christ, found in the doctrine of going the second mile, would do wonders to still argument and accusation, faultfinding and evil speaking. The same healing spirit would do wonders for the sickness of our society.

There are few stories more beautiful in all of literature than that found in the fifteenth chapter of Luke. It is the story of a heady and greedy son who demanded his inheritance and then wasted it in riotous living, rejected his father's counsel, and spurned those who loved him. When he had spent all, when he was hungry and friendless, and "when he came to himself," he turned back to his father, who, on seeing him afar off, "ran, and fell on his neck, and kissed him" (Luke 15:17, 20).

Every parent ought to read that story of a repentant son and a forgiving father again and again. It is large enough to encompass every household, and enough larger than that to encompass all humanity, for are we not all prodigal sons and daughters who need to repent and partake of the forgiving mercy of the Almighty and then follow His counsel? Have we not all made mistakes? Have we not all lived beneath ourselves from time to time? And have we not all also been in a position to extend a hand of forgiveness and fellowship?

Our Redeemer reaches out to us in forgiveness and mercy, but in so doing He commands that we repent of our wrongdoings. A true and magnanimous spirit of forgiveness will become an expression of that required repentance.

So many of us are prone to say we forgive, when in fact we are unwilling to forget. If the Almighty is willing to forget the sins of the repentant, then why are so many of us inclined to bring up the past again and again? Here is a simple but great lesson we all need to learn: There is no true forgiveness without forgetting.

Are not these words of Abraham Lincoln beautiful, which he delivered during the tragedy of a terrible civil war: "With malice toward none, with charity for all, . . . let us . . . bind up the nation's wounds."

Let us bind up the wounds—oh, the many wounds that have been caused by cutting words, by stubbornly cultivated grievances, by scheming plans to "get even" with those who may have wronged us. We all have a little of this spirit of revenge in us. Fortunately, we all also have the power to rise above it.

The willingness to forgive is a sign of spiritual and emotional maturity. It is one of the great virtues to which we all should aspire. Imagine a world filled with individuals willing both to apologize and to accept an apology. Is there any problem that could not be solved among people who possessed the humility and largeness of spirit and soul to do either—or both—when needed?

The virtues of forgiveness and mercy must frequently be exercised together. Because we live in a world where there is much harshness, hostility, and meanness, there is also much need for all of us to be more merciful.

I will never forget a young mother, a single parent who had been abandoned by her husband. With only meager skills, she was trying to earn a living and make a home for her children. Broken and discouraged, she said, with tears in her eyes, "It's a rough world out there. It's a jungle without mercy." How god-like a quality is mercy! It cannot be legislated. It must come from the heart. It must be stirred up from within. It is part of the endowment each of us receives as a son or daughter of God and a partaker of a divine birthright. I plead for an effort among all of us to give greater expression and wider latitude to this instinct that lies within us. There will likely come a time, possibly many times, within our lives when we will cry out for mercy from others. As with forgiveness, how can we expect it unless we have been merciful ourselves?

I will never forget watching on television the summary trial given a man who had been a merciless despot in an Eastern European nation. In the moment of his extremity, he wished for mercy on the part of his accusers. I know nothing of the court system under which he and his wife were tried. I know only that the hearing was short, the judgment death, and the execution quick. He had been accused of showing no mercy during long years of harsh and unrelenting oppression; now, in this hour of bitter culmination, none was extended.

A parable comes to mind:

There was a certain rich man, which was clothed in purple
and fine linen, and fared sumptuously every day: And
there was a certain beggar named Lazarus, which was laid
at his gate, full of sores, And desiring to be fed with the
crumbs which fell from the rich man's table: . . . And it
came to pass, that the beggar died, and was carried by the
angels into Abraham's bosom: the rich man also died, and
was buried; And in hell he lift up his eyes, being in tor-
ments, and seeth Abraham afar off, and Lazarus in his
bosom. And he cried and said, Father Abraham, have
mercy on me, and send Lazarus, that he may dip the tip of
his finger in water, and cool my tongue; for I am tormented in this flame. But Abraham said, Son, remember
that thou in thy lifetime receivedst thy good things, and
likewise Lazarus evil things: but now he is comforted,
and thou art tormented. And beside all this, between us
and you there is a great gulf fixed: so that they which
would pass from hence to you cannot. (Luke 16:19–26)

I plead for a stronger spirit of compassion in all of our relationships, a stronger element of mercy, for if we are merciful
we shall obtain mercy from the Ultimate Judge.

The degree to which we are able to extend mercy is evidence of our commitment to Him who is our Master. He practiced what He preached, for it was He who, while hanging on
the cross in dreadful agony, cried out, "Father, forgive them;
for they know not what they do" (Luke 23:34).

How great a thing is mercy! Most often it is quiet and
unassuming. It receives few headlines. It is the antithesis of

vengeance and hatred, of greed and egotism. Shakespeare's Portia described it this way:

> The quality of mercy is not strained,
> It droppeth as the gentle rain from heaven
> Upon the place beneath: it is twice blest;
> It blesseth him that gives, and him that takes:
> . . . it becomes
> The throned monarch better than his crown;
> His sceptre shows the force of temporal power, . . .
> But mercy is above this sceptred sway;
> It is enthroned in the hearts of kings,
> It is an attribute to God himself.

If cultivated among all men and women, the virtue of mercy would put an end to the atrocities of war. For years we have watched the conflict in Northern Ireland. Surely those who have been closest to and most affected by it must be weary of it. An outpouring of mercy on both sides would overcome the corrosive hatred that has festered for so long. There are other regions of the world where similar animosities have infuriated and uprooted people for decades, if not centuries. Oh, that each side in these conflicts might act with greater compassion toward the other! As surely as this happens, those who are merciful will find the mercy for which they hunger.

Of all the wars that have afflicted the United States, none was so costly in suffering and death, none so filled with venom and hatred as was the American Civil War. There are few more touching scenes in history than that of April 9, 1865, at Appomattox, Virginia, when General Robert E. Lee surrendered to General Ulysses S. Grant. General Grant wrote a brief statement of terms under which the soldiers of the South were free to return to their homes with their personal sidearms, their private horses, and their baggage. There was no recrimination, no demand for reparations, no apologies required or punishment given. This has gone down in the chronicles of war as a great and magnificent act of mercy.

So much of the civil strife and conflict in our society could be ameliorated by a small touch of mercy. Instead, the Mosaic law of an eye for an eye and a tooth for a tooth is often enlarged to require three eyes for one eye and three teeth for one tooth. Many victims, badgered and broken, cry in vain for a touch of kindness.

We see labor strife fraught with violence and untamed accusations. Were there a greater willingness on the part of each side to look with some element of mercy on the problems of the other, most of this could be avoided.

Our generation is afflicted with critics in the media who think they do a great and clever thing in mercilessly attacking men and women in public office and in other positions of leadership. They are prone to take a line or a paragraph out of context and pursue their prey like a swarm of killer bees. They lash out with invective and snide innuendo against those who have no effective way of fighting back or who, in the spirit of the teachings of the Master, prefer to turn the other cheek and go forward with their lives. A little mercy on the part of such critics would effect a vast change in our public communications.

The plight of the homeless is a repudiation of the greatness of our nation. It is impressive to watch those who with a compelling spirit of kindness reach out to those in distress, to help and assist, to feed and provide for, to nurture and to bless. As these extend mercy, I am confident that the God of Heaven will bless them, and their posterity after them, with His own mercy. Those who impart so generously will not lack in their own store and in their own homes, but there will be food on their tables and a roof over their heads. One cannot be merciful to others without receiving a harvest of mercy in return. It is as the Master taught: "Blessed are the merciful: for they shall obtain mercy" (Matthew 5:7).

Charles Dickens, famous for many literary masterpieces, also penned a little-known work entitled *The Life of Our Lord,* which was written originally for his own children, not for publication. In fact, during his lifetime he would not permit its publication. It was a personal thing, a simple testimony of Jesus Christ from him to them. The manuscript remained a closely held family treasure for some eighty-five years. Then his youngest son died in 1933. With the passing of that generation, the family concluded that the work might finally be published.

I was living in London in 1934 and vividly recall the advertisements of one of the popular newspapers that Dickens's *The Life of Our Lord* would be published serially. Following serialization, it was published as a book. Years later, my wife found a copy of that book and read it to our children. There are portions of his telling that I like very much, particularly the manner in which he concluded:

Remember!—It is christianity TO DO GOOD always— even to those who do evil to us. It is christianity to love our neighbour as ourself, and to do to all men as we would have them do to us. It is christianity to be gentle, merciful, and forgiving, and to keep those qualities quiet in our own hearts, and never make a boast of them, or of our prayers or of our love of God, but always to show that we love Him by humbly trying to do right in everything. If we do this, and remember the life and lessons of Our Lord Jesus Christ, and try to act up to them, we may confidently hope that God will forgive us our sins and mistakes, and enable us to live and die in Peace.

All of us love Dickens's immortal *A Christmas Carol*. But *The Life of Our Lord*, written in a very personal way, without adornment or flights of fancy, for the children he loved, carries with it a compelling admonition that has within it the power to change the world: "Remember!—It is christianity TO DO GOOD always—even to those who do evil to us."

Let us be more merciful. Let us get the arrogance out of our lives, the conceit, the egotism. Let us be more compassionate, gentler, filled with more forbearance, patience, forgiveness, and a greater measure of respect one for another. In so doing, our very example will cause others with whom we associate to be more merciful, and we shall have greater claim upon the mercy of God who in His love will be generous toward us.

Seven

Thrift and Industry:
Getting Our Houses in Order

I commend to all the virtues of industry and thrift, which I believe go hand in hand. The labor and thrift of the people make a nation, a community, or a family strong. Work and thrift make the family independent.

As a boy, I lived in what I thought was a large home. It had four rooms on the main floor—a kitchen, a dining room, a parlor, and a library. There were four bedrooms upstairs. The house stood on the corner of a large lot. There was a big lawn, with many trees that shed millions of leaves. There was an immense amount of work to be done constantly.

In my early childhood, we had a stove in the kitchen and a stove in the dining room. A furnace was later installed, and what a wonderful thing that was! But it had a voracious appetite for coal, and there was no automatic stoker. The coal had to be shoveled into the furnace and carefully banked each night.

I learned a great lesson from that monster of a furnace: If you wanted to keep warm, you had to work the shovel.

My father had the idea that his boys ought to learn to work, in the summer as well as in the winter, and so he bought a five-acre farm, which eventually grew to include more than thirty acres. We lived there all summer, and the chores never seemed to end. My father usually arose by 5:00 A.M., and we were also expected to keep an early clock. Each day, we could plan on receiving a list of jobs to be done by noon. The chores included everything from digging post holes to helping with the irrigating to working in our large orchard, where we had apple, peach, cherry, pear, and apricot trees.

At harvest time, we were expected to help bring in the fruit, something that wasn't our favorite assignment because it was sweaty, sticky work. But the fruit had to be picked, graded, packed, and sold, and all of us were needed to get the job done. Now, as I look back on that experience of my formative years, it is obvious that the farm provided a fertile environment for a number of lessons, including the fact that we can reap only what we have sown.

I believe in the gospel of work. Work is the miracle by which talent is brought to the surface and dreams become reality. There is simply no substitute under the heavens for productive labor. It is the process by which idle visions become dynamic achievements. I suppose that we are all inherently lazy. We would rather play than work. We would rather loaf than work. A little play and a little loafing are good. But it is work that spells the difference in the life of a man or a woman or a boy or a girl. Children who are taught to work and to enjoy the fruits of that labor have a great advantage as they grow toward maturity. The process of stretching our minds and utilizing the skills of our hands lifts us from the stagnation of mediocrity.

Nothing of real substance comes without work. Nothing happens in this world until there is work. Our pioneer forebears could never plow a field by turning it over in their minds. They had to put their hands to the plow and walk forward. The work is, by and large, easier now than in earlier times, but the principle is the same. There must be work, and what a great and wonderful privilege it is.

Again, there is no reason to be averse to some recreation. All work and no play makes Jack a dull boy and Jill a dull girl. But when pleasure or recreation becomes an end in itself, we are in danger. We are in trouble. We simply cannot expect to refine the substance of character from the husks of pleasures.

It has been said that the north wind made the Vikings. Hard work in the face of adversity made the American West blossom like a rose. Anyone who has traveled through Israel has marveled at the fruits of hard work properly directed. The water in the canals, the olive trees on the hillsides, the citrus groves in the valleys all bespeak the industry of men and women. Only through labor do nations become stronger, cities more attractive, families more tightly knit, and lives more robust.

I remember one weekend when my wife and I visited good friends who live in a rural community in the West. We spent one afternoon driving around the small but attractive farming town, enjoying the tidy homes and cultivated fields nearby. As we mingled with the people, it was obvious that they were unpretentious and principled. They had learned from experience that we do not reap wheat after sowing oats, that we cannot get a racehorse from a scrub mare. They knew that if we are to build another great generation, we must work with vision and with faith. The formula for success of these honest, hardworking people was inspiring to me.

Can we help but worry about the ever growing regulations in our country that seem to choke the natural initiative and ambitions of the people? Further, we now have generations of men and women who have long depended on welfare, and we see in their lives the curse of idleness and the evils of the dole. Brigham Young, the man who led a band of impoverished people across the Great Plains and the Rocky Mountains in the mid-nineteenth century and supervised the turning of what was then a desert, the Salt Lake Valley, into a prosperous region of North America, said this:

> You count me out fifty, a hundred, five hundred, or a thousand of the poorest men and women you can find in this community; with the means that I have in my possession, I will take these ten, fifty, hundred, five hundred, or a thousand people, and put them to labor; but only enough to benefit their health and to make their food and sleep sweet unto them, and in ten years I will make that community wealthy. In ten years I will put six, a hundred, or a thousand individuals, whom we have to support now by donations, not only in a position to support themselves, but they shall be wealthy, shall ride in their carriages, have fine houses to live in, orchards to go to, flocks and herds and everything to make them comfortable.

Brigham Young was able to make such a pronouncement because he had practiced what he preached.

I commend to all the virtues of industry and thrift, which I believe go hand in hand. The labor and thrift of the people make a nation, a community, or a family strong. Work and thrift make the family independent. Debt can be a terrible thing. It is so easy to incur and so difficult and laborious to repay. Borrowed money is had only at a price, and that price can be burdensome. Bankruptcy generally is the bitter fruit of debt, overextension, and uncontrolled appetites. It is a tragic culmination of a simple process of borrowing more than one can repay. I deplore waste. I deplore unnecessary and uncontrolled extravagance. I value thrift. I believe in temporal prudence and conservatism.

Benjamin Franklin, who was the same as penniless when he left home as a teenager, ultimately became one of this country's most successful Americans. In his *Autobiography*, he verified the important role that frugality and industry had played in his life:

> Remember that Time is Money. . . . Remember that Credit is Money. . . . Remember that Money is of a prolific generating Nature. . . . In short, the Way to Wealth, if you desire it, is as plain as the Way to Market. It depends chiefly on two words, Industry and Frugality; i.e., Waste neither Time nor Money, but make the best Use of both. He that gets all he can honestly, and saves all he gets (necessary Expenses excepted) will certainly become Rich; If that Being who governs the World, to whom all should look for a Blessing on their Honest Endeavours, doth not in his wise Providence otherwise determine.

Various periods of humanity's long march have been denoted as ages: the age of stone, the age of iron, the age of industry. The present age has been described, regrettably, as the age of fun. The fact is that we spend more of our money and our time trying to satisfy the physical desire for pleasure than ever before in human history. We live in the microwave generation; we expect advancements and material pleasures to come quickly and to everyone. It is an age of persuasive advertisements and skillful salesmanship, all designed to entice us to spend—and all too often to spend money we don't have.

In today's fast-paced, money-crazed society, there are attitudes regarding money and possessions about which we should all be concerned. Home equity loans and second mortgages can be had at the snap of one's fingers. Credit cards and other kinds of plastic money are available to nearly everyone over eighteen. Borrowing money is made to appear effortless and desirable, with never a mention of the responsibility to repay. Seductive advertising strives to persuade us that we deserve to have it all and to have it *now*, regardless of the cost. There is a lack of self-discipline and financial self-control that promises future doom.

The forty-first chapter of Genesis provides a compelling backdrop. Pharaoh, the ruler of Egypt, dreamed dreams that greatly troubled him. The wise men of his court could not provide an interpretation. Joseph was then brought before him.

Pharaoh said unto Joseph, In my dream, behold, I stood upon the bank of the river:

And behold, there came up out of the river seven kine, fatfleshed and well favoured; and they fed in a meadow;

And behold, seven other kine came up after them, poor and very ill favoured and lean fleshed. . . .

And the lean and the ill favoured kine did eat up the first seven fat kine: . . .

And I saw in my dream . . . seven ears came up in one stalk, full and good:

And, behold, seven ears, withered, thin, and blasted with the east wind, sprung up after them:

And the thin ears devoured the seven good ears: . . .

And Joseph said unto Pharaoh, . . . God hath shewed Pharaoh what he is about to do.

The seven good kine are seven years; and the seven good ears are seven years: the dream is one. . . .

. . . . What God is about to do he sheweth unto Pharaoh.

Behold, there come seven years of great plenty throughout all the land of Egypt:

And there shall arise after them seven years of famine. . . . And God will shortly bring it to pass. (Genesis 41:17–20, 22–26, 28–30, 32)

I want to make it clear that I am neither prophesying nor predicting years of famine in the future, but I am suggesting that the time has come to get our houses in order. Too many people are living on the very edge of their incomes or beyond.

We now witness an almost cyclical pattern of wide and fearsome swings in the markets of the world. The economy is a fragile thing. A stumble in the economy in Jakarta or Moscow can immediately affect not only investors but private citizens throughout the world. There is a portent of stormy weather ahead to which we had better give heed.

I hope with all my heart that we shall never slip into a depression. My father was a leader in our local church during the

Great Depression, and I remember how he walked the floor, worrying about the people in his care. He and his associates established an extensive wood-chopping project designed to keep the home furnaces and stoves going and the people warm in the winter. They had no money with which to buy coal. Men with good jobs suddenly found themselves out of work, and even those who had been affluent were among those who chopped wood. One family in our neighborhood lost their home because they could no longer meet the payment of eight dollars a month. It was a dark era, and many people became pessimistic and cynical as they struggled for survival.

It is impossible to appreciate the terror and insecurity that accompany such a situation unless it is experienced firsthand. I repeat: I hope we will never again see such a depression. But we ought to be troubled by the huge consumer installment debt that hangs over the people of the nation. In March 1997, that debt totaled 1.2 trillion dollars, which represented a 7 percent increase over the previous year.

Dr. James Clayton, professor of history and former dean of the graduate school at the University of Utah, has specialized, throughout his distinguished career, in the evaluation of economic history. He believes that public and private debt has become the most compelling international issue of our day. In December 1998, he explained his reasoning: "Back in the 1950s, 30 percent of [our] disposable income was debt. Now 92 percent of [our] disposable income is debt. The average American household has spent next year's entire income, and that is unprecedented in our history. Our savings rate is very, very low. A couple of weeks ago, it went below zero. That has not been true since the 1930s." He continued with a startling indictment: "Frugality is now a thing of the past, and deficit financing in the public sector and very high debt levels in the private sector [are routine]."

In January 1938, J. Reuben Clark, Jr., an international statesman who served as U.S. Ambassador to Mexico, said this:

> Interest never sleeps nor sickens nor dies; it never goes to the hospital; it works on Sundays and holidays; it never takes a vacation; it never visits nor travels; it takes no pleasure; it is never laid off work nor discharged from employment; it never works on reduced hours; . . . it is as hard and soulless as a granite cliff. Once in debt, interest is your companion every minute of the day and night; you cannot shun it or slip away from it; you cannot dismiss it; it yields neither to entreaties, demands, or orders; and whenever you get in its way or cross its course or fail to meet its demands, it crushes you.

We would all do well to review these words occasionally as a reminder of the price we pay when we borrow. I recognize that it may be necessary to borrow to get a home. But let people buy a home that they can afford and thus ease the payments that will constantly hang over their heads without mercy or respite for as long as thirty years.

Ours is a wasteful generation. Our pioneer forebears lived by the motto: "Fix it up, wear it out, make it do, or do without." Today, the obsession with riches cankers and destroys and leads to irresponsible financial decisions.

No one knows when emergencies will strike—be they natural disasters or personal crises. I think of a man who was highly successful in his profession. He lived in comfort. He built a large home. Then one day, without warning, he was involved in a serious accident and almost lost his life. He was left severely crippled, and his earning power was destroyed. He faced huge medical bills as well as other payments. In short order, he was left helpless before his creditors. One moment he was rich, the next he was broke and, consequently, a broken man.

Nothing is quite as discouraging and debilitating as debt and obligations that one cannot meet. Self-reliance cannot obtain when there is serious debt hanging over a household. One has neither independence nor freedom from bondage when obligated by debts. I am grateful to be able to say that in managing the affairs of the church I represent, we have stringently followed the practice of setting aside each year a percentage of the church's income against a possible day of need. Furthermore, our church—in all of its operations, in all of its undertakings, in all of its departments—is able to function without borrowed money. If we cannot get along, we will curtail our programs. We will shrink expenditures to fit the income. We will not borrow.

What a wonderful feeling it is to be free of debt, to have a little money put away where it can be retrieved when necessary for an emergency. I think of a number of astute individuals who have followed such a practice personally. One man told me about a mortgage he had on his home that was drawing four percent interest. Financial consultants told him it was foolish to pay off that mortgage when it carried so low a rate of interest. But the first opportunity he had to acquire some means, he and his wife determined they would pay off the mortgage. He has been free of debt since that day—which I believe has contributed, over time, to his subsequent financial comfort and, more importantly, to a sense of great personal freedom and peace of mind. I believe it is one reason that he wears a smile on his face and whistles while he works.

We have been seduced into believing that borrowed money has no penalty, that financial bondage is an acceptable way to live. I suggest that it is not. We would do well to look to the condition of our personal finances, to be modest and prudent in our expenditures, to discipline our purchasing and avoid debt to the extent possible, to pay off debt quickly, and to free ourselves from the bondage of others.

May we set our houses in order. If we have paid our debts, if we have a reserve, even though it be small, then should storms howl about our heads, we will have shelter for our families and peace in our hearts.

Work and thrift are indeed virtues to be exploited, virtues to be admired, virtues vital to the stability of any healthy society, family, and individual.

Eight

Gratitude: A Sign of Maturity

Gratitude is the beginning of civility, of decency and goodness, of a recognition that we cannot afford to be arrogant. We should walk with the knowledge that we will need help every step of the way.

It has been my pleasure to meet and mingle with some of the gifted and influential men and women of the twentieth century, but I have also walked on narrow and dirty streets where filth, poverty, and degradation abound. I have walked among the poor of the earth, the underprivileged who live constantly with the gaunt figure of hunger. I have been on the streets of Calcutta and in slum areas of South America, the Philippines, and Asia. I have witnessed the stifling, choking grasp of poverty that holds millions in its relentless clutch. I will never forget visiting an orphanage in southern India. My wife and I both struggled to hold back tears as we looked upon tiny, abandoned babies lying on wooden slats, undernourished and with little chance for life, let alone hope for the future.

These experiences have made me all the more aware of the bounties we enjoy in this land. We are truly a blessed people who live at a marvelous time in the earth's history and who enjoy a magnificent land overflowing with privileges and opportunities. Although we acknowledge that far too many people live at the edge of survival, still we must admit that never before in the history of the world has a nation or a people enjoyed such riches and liberties.

For all this and much more, we should be grateful. And we ought to express our gratitude daily in countless ways—to each other, to our parents and other family members who have contributed so dramatically to our lives, to friends who have given us the benefit of the doubt again and again, to colleagues and associates who motivate and inspire us to reach higher and do better, to prudent leaders who serve selflessly, and, particularly, to a Higher Power from Whom all ultimate blessings and goodness flow.

Gratitude is a sign of maturity. It is an indication of sincere humility. It is a hallmark of civility. And most of all, it is a divine principle. I doubt there is anything in which we more offend the Almighty than in our tendency to forget His mercies and to be ungrateful for that which He has given us.

Where there is appreciation, there is also courtesy and concern for the rights and property of others. Without these, there is arrogance and evil. Where there is gratitude, there is humility instead of pride, generosity rather than selfishness.

We would do well to get on our knees and thank the Almighty for His bounties. We would do well, also, to cultivate within ourselves a spirit of thanksgiving for the blessing of life itself and for the marvelous gifts and privileges we enjoy. The Lord has said that "the meek shall inherit the earth" (Matthew 5:5). It is difficult to escape the interpretation that, rather than an attitude of self-sufficiency, meekness implies a spirit of gratitude, an acknowledgment of a greater power beyond oneself, a recognition of God and an acceptance of His commandments and inspired way of living. Gratitude is the beginning of wisdom. Stated differently, true wisdom cannot be obtained unless it is built on a foundation of true humility and gratitude.

Indeed, gratitude is the beginning of civility, of decency and goodness, of a recognition that we cannot afford to be arrogant. We should walk with the knowledge that we will need help every step of the way. The absence of gratitude bespeaks a lack of appreciation and an ignorance that comes of an attitude of self-sufficiency. It expresses itself in ugly egotism and, frequently, in malicious conduct. Many selfish, arrogant, and usually miserable people in this world walk without gratitude. Perhaps they do so because they do not fully realize all they have to be thankful for. With this in mind, I enumerate here some of the blessings common to all of us, for which I am most grateful.

To begin with, I am grateful for the wonders of the human body and the miracle of the human mind as creations of the Almighty. I have in my home a reasonably good sound system. Now and again I sit quietly in the semidarkness and listen for an hour or so to music that has endured through the centuries because of its remarkable qualities. Every time I listen to Beethoven's concerto for the violin, I marvel that such a thing could come of the mind of a man. In many respects, the composer was much like the rest of us. He got hungry, felt pain, and had most of the problems that we all have—and perhaps some that we do not have. But out of the genius of his mind came a tremendous blending to create rare and magnificent masterpieces of music.

Have you ever contemplated the wonder of yourself, the eyes with which you see, the ears with which you hear, the voice with which you speak? No camera ever built can compare with the human eye. No method of communication ever devised can compare with the voice and the ear. No pump ever built will run as long or as efficiently as the human heart. What a remarkable creature each of us is! We can think by day and dream by night. We can speak and hear, smell and taste and feel. We can store what we experience and learn in a remarkable retrieval system unmatched by the most spectacular computer. We can learn and grow and progress and become better tomorrow than we are today.

Consider the human fingers. The most skillful attempt to reproduce a finger mechanically has brought only a crude approximation. The next time you use your fingers, look at them and sense their wonder. In a prestigious concert hall, I was seated in a location that allowed me to see the fingers of the performers in the orchestra. Every one—whether playing the strings, the percussion instruments, the brass, the woodwinds— used his or her fingers. One does not have to use one's fingers to sing or hum or whistle, but there would be little else of musical harmony without the deft action of trained fingers.

I believe the human body to be the creation of divinity. Our bodies were designed and created by the Almighty to be the tabernacles, the earthly receptacles, of our eternal spirits.

We ought to be grateful for the growing accumulation of knowledge about taking care of the body. The smoking of a single cigarette, actuarially speaking, will result in a loss of seven minutes of life for the smoker. Knowing that is so, how can any thoughtful individual make the deliberate choice to smoke? Or take debilitating drugs into his or her system? Or expose himself or herself to AIDS or to other health risks that result from abuse of the body and total disregard of one's future?

Contemplate the wonders of the age in which we live, this greatest of all ages in the history of humanity. More inventions and scientific discoveries have been made during my lifetime than in all the previous centuries of human history combined. This is the remarkable fruition of the efforts of thinking men and women who have applied their inquisitive and dedicated thought processes in the fields of medicine, industrial safety, hygiene and sanitary measures, chemistry, and research in genetics, microbiology, the environment, and other disciplines, all involving the processes of the human mind. How can we help but be grateful for such miracles?

I am grateful for this remarkable land, ravaged though it is with social problems of every order. I have stood in the American military cemetery in Suresnes, France, where are buried some who died in the First World War, including my older brother. It is a quiet and hallowed place, a remembrance of great sacrifices that were offered to "make the world safe for democracy." Time and time again, I have been up and down South Korea from the thirty-eighth parallel in the north to Pusan in the south, and have seen the ridges and the valleys where Americans fought and died, not to save their own land, but to preserve freedom for people who were strangers to them but whom they acknowledged to be brothers under the Fatherhood of God. I traveled from one end of South Vietnam to the other during those war years when 55,000 Americans, fighting in the cause of human liberty, died in the sultry, suffocating heat of that strange and foreign place. A line from Maxwell Anderson's play *Valley Forge* comes to mind. As his men prepare to bury a dead comrade, General George Washington says, almost in bitterness, "This liberty will look easy by and by when nobody dies to get it." I feel tremendous gratitude for the many thousands throughout history who have given their lives in freedom's cause.

I am grateful for those who put the welfare of others before their own comfort and success. I am grateful for our forebears and for the pioneers who laid the foundations of this great land; they endured untold hardship and personal privations and sacrifice to brave a new world where a climate of liberty and justice could prevail for all.

I am grateful for beauty. The earth in its pristine beauty is an expression of the nature of its Creator. The language of the opening chapter of Genesis is intriguing. It states that "the earth was without form, and void; and darkness was upon the face of the deep" (Genesis 1:2). Perhaps at that stage in its development it presented anything but a picture of beauty. "And God said, Let there be light: and there was light" (Genesis 1:3). From that point the Creation continued until "God saw every thing that he had made, and, behold, it was very good" (Genesis 1:31). Surely this means that it was beautiful, for "out of the ground made the Lord God to grow every tree that is pleasant to the sight" (Genesis 2:9).

I am grateful for the beauty of nature—the flowers, the fruit, the sky, the peaks and the plains from which they rise. I feel thanks for the beauty of animals. There is beauty in all peoples. I speak not of the beauty or the image that comes of lotions and creams, of pastes and packs, as seen in slick-paper magazines and on television. Whether the skin be fair or dark, the eyes round or slanted, is absolutely irrelevant. I have seen beautiful people in every one of the scores of nations I have visited. Little children everywhere are beautiful. And so are the aged, whose wrinkled hands and faces speak of struggle and survival, of the virtues and values they have embraced. We wear on our faces the results of what we believe and how we behave, and such behavior is most evident in the eyes and on the faces of those who have lived many years.

How grateful I am for beauty—the beauty of God's unspoiled creations, the beauty of His sons and daughters who walk in virtue without whimpering, meeting the challenges of each new day.

I speak at many funerals these days. Each one becomes a reminder of the brevity of life. I am grateful for strength and vitality. As a man getting along in years, looking back on the last eighty-nine and looking forward to the next ten, I appreciate the words of Robert Browning:

> Grow old along with me!
> The best is yet to be,
> The last of life, for which the first was made;
> Our times are in His hand
> Who saith, "A whole I planned,
> Youth shows but half; trust God:
> See all, nor be afraid."

For more than sixty years, my wife and I have walked together through much of storm as well as sunshine. Today, neither of us stands as tall as we once did. For both of us, the rivets are getting a little loose and the solder is getting a little soft. As I looked at her across the table one evening recently, I noted the wrinkles in her face and hands. But are they less beautiful than before? No; in fact, they are more so. Those wrinkles have a beauty of their own, and inherent in their presence is something that speaks reassuringly of strength and integrity, and a love that runs more deeply and quietly than ever before. I am thankful for the beauty that comes with age and perspective and increased understanding.

When we walk with gratitude, we do not walk with arrogance and conceit and egotism, but rather with a spirit of thanksgiving that is becoming to us and will bless our lives. We should all be thankful to the Almighty for His wonderful blessings upon us. We have all that this great age has to offer in the world. How lucky can we be, really? We ought to be grateful, to be thankful, to walk with appreciation and respect for the blessings of life and happiness that we enjoy.

Gratitude is of the very essence of worship—thanksgiving to the God of Heaven, who has given us all that we have that is good. I was always impressed with a religious leader whom I heard pray many times in the course of our association. He rarely asked for anything in his prayers. For the most part, his prayers were always expressions of gratitude for one thing after another.

Above all else, I am grateful for my belief in God and in His Beloved Son, the Redeemer of the world, the Lord Jesus Christ of the New Testament. In all of human history there is nothing to compare with the Savior's gracious gift of atoning sacrifice. I am thankful for the principle of the Golden Rule as enunciated by the Savior: "Whatsoever ye would that men should do unto you, do ye even so unto them" (Matthew 7:12).

I am grateful to be part of a society that allows all people to worship God according to the dictates of conscience, that all may worship how, where, or what they may. Recent events in China and Europe should have brought from every American a prayer of gratitude for the provisions of the Bill of Rights. Our television screens have carried into our own homes the demonstrations and cries of many people for freedom and liberty concerning basic human rights that we take for granted.

The First Amendment to our Constitution states that "Congress shall make no law respecting an establishment of religion, or prohibiting the free exercise thereof; . . . ." It is interesting to me that this is the first item on the bill of liberties demanded by the people of our fledgling nation. One who stands where I stand knows something of the constant threat of the heavy hand of government against religion. It is felt at the local level, at the state level, at the federal level. In recent years, it has grown in strength, and the attacks have increased in frequency. Religion and the free exercise thereof—how precious and treasured a boon it is!

I have the utmost gratitude for the sacred writings of the past. These books, which have lived through the centuries, set forth the basis of our civil law, our societal relationships, our family responsibilities, and, most importantly, divinely given teachings, principles, and commandments by which we may safely and confidently set the course of our lives. They enunciate the relentless law of the harvest—"as ye sow, so shall ye reap." They spell out a law of accountability under which we must someday give a report of our labors on this earth—our activities and our rewards—to the Almighty, who has granted us the privilege of life with all of its joys, its opportunities, and its challenges.

With that knowledge, I am also grateful to know of the efficacy of prayer, the invitation to appeal to a Power much greater than my own. I believe in the integrity of the New Testament promise that "if any of you lack wisdom, let him ask of God, that giveth to all men liberally, and upbraideth not; and it shall be given him" (James 1:5). I believe that God really will communicate with earnest men and women who seek Him, that none of us need face the challenges of life alone. I believe that a nation at prayer may be endowed with a unique and marvelous power, a power that comes from God, the Creator and ruler of the universe. He grants agency to humans and allows them to run their willful course, and this is the reason for our present troubles. Notwithstanding this, He can touch the hearts of His children of all lands for good, and can bring into play those forces that lead to peace and justice and human happiness.

Finally, how grateful I am for life, for a feeling of purpose, for opportunities to serve, for freedom to move about as I please, and for living in this remarkable age. I never get over the wonder of it. Surely we are a blessed people, for which we ought to express gratitude and then show the depth of that gratitude by the goodness and measure of our lives.

Nine

Optimism in the Face of Cynicism

My plea is that we stop seeking out the storms and enjoy more fully the sunlight. I am suggesting that as we go through life, we "accentuate the positive." I am asking that we look a little deeper for the good, that we still our voices of insult and sarcasm, that we more generously compliment and endorse virtue and effort.

We live in an intriguing age, a curious age in many respects, an age in which the ability and power to communicate, and therefore to influence and persuade, reign supreme. With the proliferation of technology, and the various forms of media clamoring to take advantage of it, has come an interesting side effect. It seems today that we are subjected to a constant barrage of character assassination that has nearly obscured national discussion of vital issues—issues that truly could and would improve the daily lives of men and women, boys and girls. A large factor in all of this is the media. Pick up any major daily newspaper or weekly news magazine, or turn to the news on any one of the many available channels. It is impossible to read the columns or listen to the commentaries without sensing that there is a terrible ailment of gloom in this land. We are constantly fed a steady and sour diet of pessimism, faultfinding, second-guessing, and evil speaking one of another. The pathetic fact is: Negativism sells.

Some writers of our news columns are brilliant. They are men and women of incisive language and scintillating expression. They are masters of the written and spoken word. Likewise, some television commentators are masters. But some seem unable to deal with balanced truth, notwithstanding their protests to the contrary. The attitude of many is negative. With studied art, they pour out their vinegar of invective and anger, judging as if all wisdom belonged to them. Under the guise of analysis and informed opinion, they frequently dwell on their subjects' failings rather than their strengths. If we took such pundits seriously, we might think the whole nation and indeed the whole world was going down the drain. There have been times when a particularly heavy dose of such cynicism has caused me to reflect that surely this is the age and place of the gifted pickle sucker!

A sustained diet of a negative point of view has serious repercussions. The negative becomes the stuff of headlines and long broadsides that in many cases are caricatures of the facts. This spirit of negativism grows and begins to hang as a cloud over the land, providing a misleading portrait of the facts and, in the process, reaching down to the individual man and woman and influencing attitudes, outlook, and even values.

The tragedy is that the spirit is epidemic. Read the letters to the editor in almost any daily newspaper. Some of them are filled with venom, written by people who seem to find no good in the world or in their associates. To hear tell, *nowhere* is there a person of integrity holding public office. Businesspeople are *all* crooks. The utilities are out to *rob* the public. The snide remark, the sarcastic jibe, the cutting down of associates—these too often are the essence of our conversation. Closer to home, husbands chafe, wives weep, and children finally give up under the barrage of criticism leveled by family members at each other. Criticism is the forerunner of divorce, the cultivator of rebellion, the catalyst that accelerates to failure.

It will do us no good to be naïve about the challenges we face in this country. We *do* have problems, and they are not a few. There *are* issues that demand our earnest, inspired attention. But there is too much fruitless carping and criticism of America. What might become of this land if we spoke less of its weaknesses and more of its goodness and strength, its capacity and potential? Without doubt, we shall have days of trial. So long as we have more politicians than statesmen, we shall have problems. But if we will turn our time and talents away from vituperative criticism, away from constantly looking for evil, and will emphasize instead the greater good, America will continue to go forward with the blessing of the Almighty and stand as an ensign of strength and peace and generosity to all the world. This is a great land, a choice land, a chosen land.

I am an optimist! What a wonderful time it is to be alive, here at the turn of a milestone century! With that frame of reference, my plea is that we stop seeking out the storms and enjoy more fully the sunlight. I am suggesting that as we go through life, we "accentuate the positive." I am asking that we look a little deeper for the good, that we still our voices of insult and sarcasm, that we more generously compliment and endorse virtue and effort.

I am not recommending that all criticism be silent. Growth comes with correction. Strength comes of change and repentance. Wise is the man or woman who, having committed mistakes now pointed out by others, changes his or her course. I am not suggesting that our conversation be all sweetness and honey. Clever expression that is sincere and honest is a skill to be sought and cultivated. What I am suggesting is that we have had missing from our society a buoyant spirit of optimism. What I am asking is that we turn from the negativism that so permeates our culture and look for the remarkable good in the land and times in which we live; that we speak of one another's virtues more than we speak of one another's faults; that optimism replace pessimism; that uncertainty and worry be pushed aside by an enduring feeling of hope.

When I was a young man and was prone to speak critically, my wise father would say: "Cynics do not contribute, skeptics do not create, doubters do not achieve." Looking at the dark side of things always leads to a spirit of pessimism, which often leads to defeat. Let us replace our fears with faith.

If ever there was a man who achieved this, who rallied a nation in its time of deepest distress, it was Winston Churchill. The German juggernaut had overrun Austria, Czechoslovakia, France, Belgium, Holland, and Norway, and was moving into Russia. Bombs were falling on London. Most of Europe was in the dread grasp of tyranny, and England was to be next. In that dangerous hour, when the hearts of those around him were failing, this great English-man gave a speech for the ages. He said, in part:

> Do not let us speak of darker days; let us speak rather of sterner days. These are not dark days: these are great days—the greatest days our country has ever lived; and we must all thank God that we have been allowed, each of us according to our stations, to play a part in making these days memorable in the history of our race.

Following the terrible catastrophe of the defeat at Dunkirk, the prophets of doom foretold the end of Britain. But in that dark and solemn hour, I personally heard this re-markable man say these words as they were broadcast across America:

> We shall not flag or fail. . . . We shall fight in France, we shall fight on the seas and oceans, we shall fight with growing confidence and growing strength in the air, we shall defend our Island, whatever the cost may be, we shall fight on the beaches, we shall fight on the landing grounds, we shall fight in the fields and in the streets, we shall fight in the hills; we shall never surrender.

Talk such as this, and not the critical faultfinding of glib cynics, saw victory distantly through the dark clouds of war, preserved the great people of Britain through those dark and deadly days, and saved the United Kingdom from catastro-phe. We are creatures of our thinking. We can talk ourselves into defeat, or we can talk ourselves into victory. Churchill is just one example, albeit a superb and convincing one, of the prevailing power of optimism and hope.

More recently, we witnessed another dramatic and dynamic period in human history when the barriers separating eastern and western Europe fell, and the iron fist of despotism was shattered. A new day dawned over a vast region of the world. During subsequent years, it has become apparent that the oppression of so long a period cannot be lifted in a day; nonetheless, a new light shines over the eastern regions. What a wonderful season it is to be alive! How inspiring it was to listen to Mikhail Gorbachev's speeches, in which there was little evidence of negativism. His words were those of a man with confidence, with optimism, with the assurance that comes of knowing one is doing the right thing.

We all tend to worry about the future. And yes, there may be lean days ahead for many of us. There will doubtless be challenges of all varieties. No one can avoid them all. But we must not despair or give up. We must look for the sunlight through the clouds.

As mentioned earlier, I lived through the most serious economic depression of modern times. Heaven forbid that we should ever slip again into the financial quagmire of the thirties! Those were days of long soup lines, of suicides that came of discouragement, of a bleakness of life that is incomprehensible to those who didn't experience it. Despite the prevailing cynicism, somehow we survived and stayed alive. We worked at whatever employment we could find, though the pay was meager. But we managed to eat and keep going. In time, opportunities opened here and there. We moved forward with faith in the Almighty, which cultivated a spirit of optimism. In 1982, I attended the fiftieth anniversary party of my university's graduating class and was there reunited with men and women who had become prominent in many undertakings. They had become leaders. They had looked for the positive in life, praying with faith and working with diligence. Despite overwhelming odds, they had moved forward with a spirit of optimism and a willingness to work as hard as they could.

Regardless of our circumstances, we must do the same—go forward with faith and prayer, calling on the Lord for His sustenance and direction. We will discover, as the years pass, that there has been a subtle guiding of our footsteps in paths of progress and great purpose.

We must not be trapped by the sophistry of the world, which for the most part is negative and which seldom, if ever, bears good fruit. We must not be ensnared by or lean on the words of those clever ones whose self-appointed mission is to demean that which is sacred, to emphasize human weakness rather than inspired strength, and to undermine faith.

We must walk with hope and faith. We must speak affirmatively and cultivate an attitude of confidence. We all have the capacity to do so. Our strength will give strength to others, and the cumulative, rippling effect will be tremendous.

How magnificently and munificently we have been blessed! One does not have to travel far, nor to experience much of what the world has to offer, to see how richly we have been endowed in this great country. With gratitude in our hearts, let us stop dwelling on the problems we have, other than in a spirit of contribution to solutions. Let us rather count our blessings and determine to do all we can to make this world a better place.

In our individual circumstances, let us look for and cultivate the wonders of our opportunities. We can be overcome by
a spirit of defeatism, or we can eagerly embrace opportunities
to learn, to develop marvelous associations, and to build great
loyalties.

On one occasion when the Savior was walking among a
crowd, a woman who had been ill for a long time touched His
garment. He perceived that strength had gone out of Him.
The strength that was His had strengthened her. So it may be
with each of us. Rather than making cutting remarks one to
another, could we not cultivate the art of complimenting, of
strengthening, of encouraging? What wonders we can accomplish when others have faith in us! No leader can long succeed
in any society without the confidence of the people. It is so
with us in our daily associations.

Responsibilities have been divinely laid on each of us, and
they are incumbent on anyone who wishes to live in an orderly,
peaceful society: to bear one another's burdens, to strengthen
one another, to encourage one another, to lift one another, to
look for the good in one another, and to emphasize that good.
There is not a man or woman who cannot become depressed on
the one hand, or lifted on the other, by the remarks of his or her
associates.

Columnist Sydney Harris once published these memorable
observations:

Sir Walter Scott was a trouble to all his teachers and so was
Lord Byron. Thomas Edison, as everyone knows, was considered a dullard in school. Pestalozzi, who later became

Italy's foremost educator, was regarded as wild and foolish by his school authorities. Oliver Goldsmith was considered almost an imbecile. The Duke of Wellington failed in many of his classes. Among famous writers, Burns, Balzac, Boccaccio, and Dumas made poor academic records. Flaubert, who went on to become France's most impeccable writer, found it extremely difficult to learn to read. Thomas Aquinas, who had the finest scholastic mind of all Catholic thinkers, was actually dubbed "the dumb ox" at school. Linnaeus and Volta did badly in their studies. Newton was last in his class. Sheridan, the English playwright, wasn't able to stay in one school more than a year.

Like those famous people mentioned, many of our forebears and those who built the foundations of this land were imperfect. They were human. They doubtless made mistakes and fell short from time to time. But the mistakes were minor when compared with the marvelous work they accomplished. To highlight the mistakes of a person and gloss over the greater good is to draw a caricature. Caricatures are amusing, but they are often ugly and dishonest. A man may have a wart on his cheek and still have a face of beauty and strength, but if the wart is emphasized unduly in relation to his other features, the portrait is lacking in integrity.

There was only one perfect man who ever walked the earth. The Lord uses imperfect people—you and me—to build strong societies. If some of us occasionally stumble, or if our characters may have been slightly flawed in one way or another, the wonder is the greater that we accomplish so much.

A young couple came to see me a while ago. Six months earlier, they had been married. They had declared their love one for another. They had pledged their loyalty one to another. Now, the young man came to my office disillusioned, bitter, and heartbroken. His wife, he said, did this and that—simple little things of small consequence, such as leaving the dishes undone when she left for work in the morning. And nothing seemed to make her happy. Then his wife came in, a beautiful girl of great talent. She spoke of her husband's faults. He was stingy. He did not pick up his clothes. He was careless. Each had his or her faults, every one of which was easily correctable. The problem lay in the fact that these two had a stronger inclination to emphasize each other's faults than to talk of their respective virtues. With a little discipline, each could have changed. With a little desire, each could have spoken with a different tone. But neither was willing. They had permitted a negative attitude and outlook to destroy the sweetest, richest association of life. They had thrown away with careless and sour words the hopes and dreams of eternity. With criticism and shouting, they had violated the most sacred of all relationships.

Criticism and pessimism destroy families, undermine institutions of all kinds, defeat nearly everyone, and spread a shroud of gloom over entire nations. We must resist partaking of the spirit of our times. We need rather to look for the good all about us. There is so much that is sweet and decent and good upon which to build. Above and beyond the negative, the critical, the cynical, and the doubtful, we can and must learn to look to the positive and the affirmative.

We have so much to live for, so much to hope for! Humanity is essentially good. We are all of one great family. We can give strength to the voice of hope. We can give thanks to those who work for peace. We can give added attention to those who feed the hungry and bind up the wounds of conflict. To the extent we cultivate this virtue of optimism, we will bless all the world's peoples.

Ten

Faith: Our Only Hope

Great buildings were never constructed on uncertain
foundations. Great causes were never brought to success by
vacillating leaders. Faith has always been, and always must be,
at the root of any meaningful practice and endeavor.

I f there is any one thing that you and I need, to help us find
success and fulfillment in this world, it is faith—that dynamic, powerful, marvelous element by which, as Paul declared, the very worlds were framed (see Hebrews 11:3). I refer
not to some ethereal concept but to a practical, pragmatic,
working faith—the kind of faith that moves us to get on our
knees and plead with the Lord for guidance, and then, having
a measure of divine confidence, get on our feet and go to work
to help bring the desired results to pass. Such faith is an asset
beyond compare. Such faith is, when all is said and done, our
only genuine and lasting hope.

Faith is so much more than a theological platitude,
though many regard it as such. It is a fact of life. Faith can
become the very wellspring of purposeful living. There is no

more compelling motivation to worthwhile endeavor than the knowledge that we are children of God, that God expects us to do something with our lives, and that He will give us help when help is sought.

Could not any of us say that if we had greater faith in God we could do better than we are now doing? There is no obstacle too great, no challenge too difficult, if we have faith. With faith we can rise above those negative elements in our lives that constantly pull us down. With effort we can develop the capacity to subdue those impulses that lead to degrading and evil actions. With faith we can school our appetites. We can reach out to those who are discouraged and defeated, and we can warm them by the strength and power of our own faith.

Some years ago, my wife and I were aboard a plane flying between Honolulu and Los Angeles. At that time, only propeller-driven aircraft were available. About midway across the Pacific, one of the motors stopped. There was a decrease in speed, a lowering in altitude, and a certain amount of nervousness among all of us on board. Much of the aircraft's power was missing, and the hazards were increased accordingly. Without that power, we could not fly high, fast, or safely. What a welcome sight was the Los Angeles airport when we finally reached it!

It is so with our lives when we discount the need for faith and disregard knowledge of the Lord. Under those conditions, we are, as it were, flying on partial power. We simply cannot do as much alone as we can when we team our efforts with the Divine. Passive acceptance or acknowledgment of God is not enough. Vibrant testimony comes of anxious seeking.

So, when I discuss faith, I do not mean it in an abstract sense. I mean it as a living, vital force that comes with recognition of God as our Father and Jesus Christ as our Savior. To those who accept this basic premise, there will come an acceptance of the scriptural teachings and an obedience that will bring peace and joy in this life.

Our lives are the only meaningful expression of what we believe and in Whom we believe. And the only real wealth, for any of us, lies in our faith. Why do I say this? Faith in a Divine Being, in the Almighty, is *the* great moving power that can change our lives. With it comes the only lasting comfort and peace of mind. God is our Eternal Father, and He lives. I don't understand the wonder of His majesty; I can't comprehend His glory. But I know that He is intensely interested in our welfare and involved in our lives, that I can speak with Him in prayer, and that He will hear and listen.

I am impressed with Commander William Robert Anderson, the man who took the submarine *Nautilus* under the North Pole from the waters of the Pacific to the waters of the Atlantic. In his wallet he carried a tattered card with these words: "I believe I am always divinely guided. I believe I will always take the right road. I believe that God will always make a way, even when there appears to be no way." I share his convictions, for I too believe that God will always make a way, even when there appears to be no way.

Faith in something greater than ourselves enables us to do what we have said we'll do, to press forward when we are tired or hurt or afraid, to keep going when the challenge seems overwhelming and the course is entirely uncertain. As a boy, I was stirred by Joaquin Miller's poem "Columbus":

129

Behind him lay the great Azores,
Behind the Gates of Hercules:
Before him not the ghost of shores,
Before him only shoreless seas.
The good mate said, "Now must we pray,
For lo! The very stars are gone.
Brave Adm'r'l, speak; what shall I say?"
"Why, say: 'Sail on! Sail on! And on!'"
Then, pale and worn, he kept his deck,
And peered through darkness. Ah, that night
Of all dark nights! And then a speck—
A light! A light! A light! A light!
It grew, a starlit flag unfurled!
It grew to be Time's burst of dawn.
He gained a world; he gave that world
Its grandest lesson: "On! Sail on!"

Columbus kept his trust; he kept his faith. And he discovered a hemisphere.

I think of Lord Nelson on the morning of the Battle of Trafalgar, when he said, "England expects every man to do his duty." After that fierce and bloody contest, as he stood on the deck of his ship to extend humanity to his enemy, a ball was fired within fifteen yards of where he stood. He fell to the deck, his spine shattered. Three and a quarter hours later he died, his last articulated words being, "Thank God. I have done my duty!" A tall shaft and statue stand in his honor in Trafalgar Square in London. What that statue honors is a man who was true to himself, true to his country, true to what he had said he would do—all of which is made possible by faith.

Faith and willingness to believe will chase pessimism away and replace it with hope and confidence. It is a source of immense personal comfort and peace of mind to have the knowledge that God is with us, and that even when there is no way—perhaps particularly when there appears to be no way—He will open the way.

Said the Lord in a dark and troubled hour to those he loved, "Let not your heart be troubled, neither let it be afraid" (John 14:27). Faith cannot grow or be exercised in an environment of doubt.

We live in complicated and confusing times. Frequently, we find ourselves in positions where it is not easy to face up to that which is expected of us, or to stand up for what we know and believe to be true. We need more faith. We should know that the Almighty will not give us requirements or commandments beyond our power to observe. He will not ask us to do things for which we lack the capacity. Our problem lies in our fears and in our appetites.

Without preservation and cultivation of the things spiritual, our material success will be as ashes in our mouths. The spirit is as much a part of a person as is the body, and it too needs nourishment—the nourishment born of faith in and devotion to a Supreme Being. This is the source that gives refinement to humans, that lifts them above the plane of the animals in the jungle, that motivates their finest deeds, that is divine in its essence. In the headlong materialistic rush in which the world is engaged, such faith is being strangled and trampled. If we are not careful, with it will go our liberty, the dignity of the individual, the altruism that makes life livable, the peace for which we long. We cannot survive without faith.

I have not forgotten an editorial written some years ago on this topic in which the following sentiment was expressed: "If America is to grow great, we must stop gagging over the word 'spiritual.' Our task is to rediscover and reassert our faith in the non-utilitarian values on which American life has rested from its beginning."

A provocative *Wall Street Journal* article, published one Christmas Eve, stated:

> As we gather . . . to celebrate the most famous holiday of our long-dominant religious faith, the very idea of religion finds itself under siege. The word of God . . . dare not be heard in the nation's schools. The creche cannot be erected on public property; for the first time since the conversion of Constantine, the state has outlawed the display of Christian symbols. Meanwhile schools distribute condoms, even over the objections of parents. . . . Christianity has instructed us on moral issues for two millenniums, and Judaism longer still. With or without personal faith, we have been living off this capital. . . . Rather than denigrating Christianity and religion in general, socially conscious elites ought to be asking what the religious impulse can teach us, and how amid the winds of modernity we might start to replenish the stock of moral guidance it bequeathed us.

I believe that. I believe it not only for America but for all nations. I commend it for thoughtful consideration. I am convinced that no nation can for long base its progress solely on materialism, military might, and scientific advancement. We need—oh, how we need—to reintroduce the Almighty and His influence into our lives.

Great buildings were never constructed on uncertain foundations. Great causes were never brought to success by vacillating leaders. Faith has always been, and always must be, at the root of any meaningful practice and endeavor. Theology may be argued over, but personal testimony coupled with performance cannot be refuted.

Several years ago, columnist Cal Thomas in the *Los Angeles Times* wrote an interesting piece under the headline, "While Americans Throw Religion Out of Schools, Russians Want It Back." He described successful attempts to remove anything religious from public schools in the United States, contrasting them with an invitation from Russia to bring teachers and Bibles to their country's public schools to "restore the value and ethical base they believe their children lost during seven decades of atheistic indoctrination." He summarized:

What could be more ironic? Americans are doing what they can to wipe out religion from public schools, while Russians are doing what they can to revive religion in their public schools. Having been without religious freedom for most of this century, Russians apparently see the value of what they lost. Their country having been established on the principles of religious values and expression, Americans flirt with paganism, unaware of what it is like to live in an anti-religious nation. It appears the Russians have learned something from us. It also appears we have learned nothing from them.

Neglect not the cultivation of the spiritual. To do so is to eventually reap bitter fruit. The Master made this simple but profound statement that strikes at the heart of our priorities and sense of purpose: "What shall it profit a man though he gain the whole world and lose his own soul, or what shall a man give in exchange for his soul?" (Mark 8:36–37).

We must labor for the peace that comes only as we recognize, accept, and have faith in the Prince of Peace. Let us not, in our supposed sophistication and pride, our advanced learning and accomplishments, become so arrogant that we no longer feel a dependence on Him Who is greater than us all. When all else fails, the Lord is there to help us. He has issued a stunning invitation and promise, "Come unto me, all ye that labour and are heavy laden, and I will give you rest" (Matthew 11:28). Each of us has burdens. Each of us has challenges and confusing options. For each of us, there are days when things don't work out. But the Lord will help us—each one of us— carry our burdens and meet our challenges. To bring that about, however, we must believe, we must have faith that He has the power to help us, and that He *will* help us.

Strength to do battle—whether the battle against destructive habits, or the battle toward personal purity, or the battle to strengthen one's family in a world that seems increasingly less committed to the family—begins with enlisting the strength of God. He is the source of all true power. It is as though Paul understood our day when he declared: "Be strong in the Lord, and the power of his might. Put on the whole armour of God, that ye may be able to stand against the wiles of the devil. For we wrestle not against flesh and blood, but against principalities, against power, against the rulers of the darkness of this world, against spiritual wickedness in high places. Wherefore take unto you the whole armour of God, that ye may be able to withstand in the evil day, and having done all, to stand" (Ephesians 6:10–13).

It is precisely to address the struggle Paul identified that I return to a subject that I believe would do more than any other single thing to strengthen us for the inevitable challenges ahead. It is a time-honored and time-tested but increasingly neglected principle: the practice of prayer. Private devotions are disappearing from our society. Are we forgetting the Almighty, who in times of last resort is our greatest strength?

I believe in prayer. We cannot be successful alone. We desperately need the help of Someone far wiser, far more powerful than we are. I believe in the concept of speaking with our Eternal Father in the name of His Son. "Behold," he said, "I stand at the door and knock; if any man hear my voice, and open the door, I will come in to him, and will sup with him, and he with me" (Revelation 3:20). This is His invitation, and the related promise is sure.

Many of the good people of the world pray. But the trouble with many of our prayers is that we give them as if we were picking up the telephone and ordering groceries—we place our order and hang up. We need to meditate, contemplate, think of what we are praying about and for, and then speak to the Lord as one person speaks to another. "Come now, and let us reason together, saith the Lord" (Isaiah 1:18). That is the invitation. Believe in the power of prayer. It is real, it is wonderful, it is tremendous.

I was in Europe a number of years ago at a time when tanks were rolling down the streets of a great city, and students were being slaughtered with machine-gun fire. I stood that December day in the railroad station in Berne, Switzerland. At eleven o'clock in the morning, every church bell in Switzerland began to ring, and at the conclusion of that ringing, every vehicle stopped—every car on a highway, every bus, every railroad train. The great, cavernous railway station became deathly still. I looked out the front door across the plaza. Men working on the hotel opposite stood on the scaffolding with bared heads. Every bicycle stopped. Men, women, and children dismounted and stood with bared, bowed heads. Then, after three minutes of prayerful silence, great convoys of trucks laden with supplies of food, clothing, and medicine began to roll from Geneva and Berne and Basel and Zurich toward the suffering nation to the east. The gates of Switzerland were thrown open to refugees.

As I stood there that chilly winter morning, I felt the warmth and the tremendous sense of security of a nation appealing together to God. I marveled at the miraculous contrast of the oppressive power mowing down students in one nation, and the spirit of a Christian people in another who bowed their heads in prayer and reverence—and then rolled up their sleeves to provide succor and salvation.

Of all the great and wonderful and inspiring promises I have read, among the most reassuring is the unparalleled invitation of the Savior: "Ask, and it shall be given you; seek, and ye shall find; knock, and it shall be opened unto you" (Matthew 7:7). Let us never forget to pray. God lives. He is near. He is real. He is not only aware of us but cares for us. He is our Father. He is accessible to all who will seek Him.

The marvelous thing about prayer is that it is personal, it is individual, it is the most intimate communication between us and our Father. We should not hesitate to ask Him to bless us, to help us realize our righteous ambitions. We can ask Him for the important things that mean so much to us in life. He stands ready to help, strengthen, and comfort.

I think of a young man who was drafted to serve in the armed services. He was a religious boy from a home where prayer was a part of everyday life, and he thought nothing of dropping to his knees before bedtime—even in his barracks. As might be expected, the other young soldiers made fun of him, and the problem was further aggravated when he chose not to participate in some of their more raucous weekend activities off base. As a result, he soon became the brunt of many jokes and jibes. In an attempt to gain their friendship, he finally agreed one evening to go into town for a wild evening. But as they rode the bus into town, there came into his mind's eye a picture. He saw the kitchen of his home. It was suppertime. There was his family, kneeling at the kitchen chairs—his father, mother, two sisters, and a younger brother. It was as though he could hear what his little brother was saying in his prayer: "Please bless my older brother and help him come home to us safe." That mental picture did it for the young soldier. He turned away from the crowd and from activities that would have violated his personal standards. The power of prayer, particularly a pattern of prayer observed in a family, had reached across an ocean.

Daily prayer in the homes of the nation would, in just one generation, lift our heads above the flood that is engulfing us. I feel satisfied that there is no adequate substitute for the morning and evening practice of kneeling together before the Lord—father, mother, and children.

In 1872, Colonel Thomas L. Kane of Philadelphia visited the Utah territory with his wife and two sons. They traveled by wagon some three hundred miles to the southern part of the state, stopping each night in the homes of the people in the frontier settlements along the way. Mrs. Kane wrote a series of letters to her father back home. In one of them, she said:

> At every one of the places we stayed on this journey we had prayers immediately after the dinner–supper, and prayers again before breakfast. No one was excused. . . . The [people] kneel at once while the head of the household, or an honored guest prays aloud. . . . They spend very little time in ascriptions, but ask for what they need, and thank Him for what He has given. . . . [They] take it for granted that God knows our familiar names and titles, and will ask a blessing on [a particular individual by name]. I liked this when I became used to it.

It was so in the pioneer homes across this land. With the faith that came of these daily invocations, those who pioneered the great American West grubbed the sagebrush, led the waters in irrigation ditches to the parched soil, made the desert blossom as the rose, governed their families in love, lived in peace one with another and with the world, and made their names immortal as they lost themselves in the service of God.

We cannot pray in our public schools, but we can pray in our homes, and in so doing we shall reweave into the character of our children the moral strength that will become the fiber of a better society. "Seek ye the Lord while he may be found" (Isaiah 55:6).

The rewards of such a practice may not be immediately or readily apparent. They may be extremely subtle. But they will be real, for God "is a rewarder of them that diligently seek him" (Hebrews 11:6). And as we change ourselves and our children, developing within them a new respect, a spirit of gratitude, a becoming humility, we shall reform our society.

No other practice will have so salutary an effect on our lives as will the practice of kneeling together in prayer. The very words "Our Father in Heaven" have a tremendous effect. We cannot speak them with sincerity and with recognition without having some feeling of accountability to God.

Our daily conversations with Him will bring peace into our hearts and a joy into our lives that can come from no other source. Our relationships of all kinds will sweeten through the years. Our appreciation for one another will grow.

Our children will be blessed with a sense of security that comes of living in a home where dwells a wonderful, peaceful spirit. They will know and love parents who respect one another. They will experience the security of kind words quietly spoken. They will be sheltered by a father and mother who, living honestly with God, live honestly with one another and with their neighbors. They will mature with a sense of appreciation, having heard their parents, in prayer, express gratitude for blessings great and small. They will grow in their faith.

What a wonderful thing it is to remember before the Lord those who are sick and in sorrow, those who are hungry and destitute, those who are lonely and afraid, those who are in bondage and sore distress. When such prayers are uttered in sincerity, there will follow a greater desire to reach out to those in need.

It is a significant thing to teach children how to pray concerning their own needs. As members of the family kneel together in supplication to the Almighty and speak with Him of their needs, there will be distilled into the hearts of the children a natural inclination in times of distress and extremity to turn to God as their Father and their friend.

Let prayer, night and morning, as a family and as individuals, become a practice in which children grow while yet young. It will bless their lives forever.

A man I have long admired wrote this to his grandchildren concerning the family prayer of his own home: "We have not gone to bed before kneeling in prayer to supplicate divine guidance and approval. Differences may arise in the best governed families, but they will be dissipated by . . . the spirit of prayer. . . . Its very psychology tends to promote the more righteous life among men. It tends to unity, love, forgiveness, to service."

I believe deeply in the fundamental principle that each of us is a child of God. It matters not the race. It matters not the slant of our eyes or the color of our skin, the size of our bank accounts, or the prominence of our standing in society. Each of us is a son or daughter of the Almighty, Who loves us and stands ready to listen to our pleadings and help us with our problems.

Am I asking too much? Am I getting into a field where I do not belong, when I take the liberty of suggesting that the time has come for all of us to acknowledge our failures and our weaknesses and to get on our knees and seek the wisdom of Heaven?

The marvelous thing is that it works. I have seen it. I have experienced it. I am a witness to the power of prayer.

I spoke one day to a friend who had escaped from his native land. With the fall of his nation, he had been arrested and interned. His wife and children had been able to get away, but for three years and more he had been a prisoner without means of communication with those he loved. The food had been wretched, and the living conditions were oppressive, with no prospects for improvement.

"What sustained you through all those dark days?" I asked him. He responded, "My faith. My faith in Jesus Christ. I put my burdens on Him, and then they seemed so much the lighter."

The problems we face in our individual lives, in our families, and in our nation are greater than any of us can solve with our own wisdom. They are problems for which we need inspiration and spiritual guidance. The things of God are understood by the spirit of God. What we all need is the motivating and powerful spiritual inspiration that can come into the lives of those who seek it.

Are we so arrogant in our sophisticated, technologically saturated, wealthy society that we no longer feel it necessary to appeal to the God of Heaven for help, for wisdom, for comfort, and for peace? There is no room for such arrogance in the lives of any of us. Such conceit is deadly. It is self-destructive. Humility is more becoming.

When the Risen Lord appeared to His apostles, Thomas was absent. When his colleagues told him they had seen the Lord, he responded, like so many then and now, "Except I shall see in his hands the print of the nails, and put my finger into the print of the nails, and thrust my hand into his side, I will not believe" (John 20:25).

Have we not all heard others speak as Thomas spoke? "Give us," they say, "the empirical evidence. Prove before our very eyes, and our ears, and our hands, else we will not believe." This is the language of the time in which we live. Thomas the Doubter has become the example of people in all ages who refuse to accept other than that which they can physically prove and explain—as if they could prove love, or faith, or even such physical phenomena as electricity.

Continuing with the narrative, eight days later, the apostles were together again, Thomas included. "Then came Jesus, the doors being shut, and stood in the midst, and said, Peace be unto you." Singling out Thomas, He said: "Reach hither thy finger, and behold my hands; and reach hither thy hand, and thrust it into my side: and be not faithless, but believing" (John 20:26–27).

To all who have doubts, I recommend the words Thomas heard as he felt the wounded hands of the Lord: "Be not faithless, but believing." Believe in Jesus Christ, the Son of God, the greatest figure of time and eternity. Believe that He was the Creator of the earth on which we live.

Can anyone who has walked beneath the stars at night, can anyone who has seen the touch of spring upon the land doubt the hand of Divinity in creation? Observing the beauties of the earth, one is wont to speak as did the Psalmist: "The heavens declare the glory of God; and the firmament sheweth his handywork. Day unto day uttereth speech, and night unto night sheweth knowledge" (Psalm 19:1–2). All of the earth's beauty bears the fingerprint of the Master Creator.

Believe in Jehovah, He whose finger wrote upon the tablets of stone amid the thunders of Sinai, "Thou shalt have no other gods before me" (Exodus 20:3). The Decalogue, which is the basis of all good law governing human relations, is the product of His divine genius. As we look upon the vast body of legalisms designed to protect humanity and society, pause and know that it has its roots in those few brief and timeless declarations given by the all-wise Jehovah to Moses, the leader of Israel.

Believe in the sacred word of God, the Holy Bible, with its treasury of inspiration and sacred truths. Believe in yourself and your fellow human beings as sons and daughters of God, men and women with unlimited potential to do good in the world. Believe in our power to discipline ourselves against the evils that could destroy us. Every man and woman, boy and girl, has a divine inheritance. What a marvelous birthright that is!

Admittedly, I am a churchman. You would expect this kind of discussion of me. But I wish to say that respect and reverence for the Almighty and faith in His goodness and power, combined with observance of His commandments embodied within the virtues we have identified, will do more than all else to keep our ship of state on a steady course and ensure progress in the communities of America. And family prayer, which is such a natural outgrowth of our faith, will fortify and strengthen us and our families against the deceptions, distractions, and discouragements of today's society.

There is no greater thing we could do than to increase our faith in the Almighty, and to appeal to Him regularly through personal and family prayer.

PART TWO

The Guardians
of Virtue

The health of any society, the happiness of its people,
their prosperity and peace, all find their roots in the
strength and stability of the family.

Marriage

What God Hath
Joined Together

It is one thing to talk about the importance and sanctity of marriage, and another thing entirely to create such a marriage, day in and day out. Marriage can be fragile. It requires nurture and time and very much effort.

While riding in an airplane some time ago, I picked up a copy of a popular national magazine. As I thumbed through it, I came to a section titled "Strictly Personals" and counted 159 advertisements placed by lonely people seeking partners. Those who had placed the ads had labored to cast themselves in the best possible light. But it was easy to sense that behind the witty and clever descriptions were sadness, loneliness, and a great desire to find an amiable companion with whom to walk the road of life.

My heart reaches out to those who long for marriage and cannot seem to find it. Such desires are natural and God-given, for the security and peace of mind that are possible in marriage are much more difficult, perhaps even impossible, to find alone or anywhere else.

Because of my long-standing ecclesiastical assignment, I have been authorized and privileged to perform hundreds of marriages. One experience stands apart from many others. On that day, in two separate, consecutive ceremonies, I performed the marriages of two beautiful young women who were twins, each to a handsome and able young man of her choice. That evening, a double wedding reception was held, and hundreds of friends came to express their love and good wishes.

What made these weddings particularly memorable was that these beautiful girls were my granddaughters. I confess that this old grandfather choked up and had a difficult time completing the ceremonies. I am always curious about such emotion. It was a happy occasion, a fulfillment of dreams and prayers. Perhaps my tears were really an expression of joy and gratitude to God for these lovely brides and their handsome young husbands. In sacred promises, they pledged their love and loyalty and faithfulness and devotion to one another.

How wonderful a thing is marriage, a plan provided in the Almighty's wisdom for the happiness and security of His children and the continuity of the race. He is our Creator, and He designed marriage from the beginning. At the time of Eve's creation, "Adam said, This is now bone of my bones, and flesh of my flesh: . . . Therefore shall a man leave his father and his mother, and shall cleave unto his wife: and they shall be one flesh" (Genesis 2:23–24). As Paul wrote, "Neither is the man without the woman, neither the woman without the man, in the Lord" (1 Corinthians 11:11). Surely no one familiar with holy writ can doubt the divinity in the institution of marriage.

The marriage relationship encompasses the most sacred of all partnerships. The sweetest and most reassuring feelings of life, the most generous and satisfying impulses of the human heart, find expression in a marriage that stands pure and unsullied above the evils of the world. Such a marriage is the desire—the hoped-for, the longed-for, the prayed-for desire—of men and women everywhere.

I first learned of married love from the example of my own parents. We knew that our father loved our mother. I have no recollection of ever hearing him speak unkindly to her or of her. He encouraged her in her individual pursuits and in neighborhood and civic responsibilities. She had much native talent, and he urged her to use it. Her comfort was his constant concern. She likewise encouraged him and did everything in the world to make him happy. We looked upon our parents as equals—companions who worked together and loved and appreciated one another as they loved us.

At the age of fifty, my mother developed cancer. My father was solicitous of her every need. I still vividly remember the prayers we had as a family during her illness, with his tearful pleadings and ours.

It was nearly seventy years ago, but I can still picture with clarity the image of my brokenhearted father as he stepped off the train and greeted us, his grief-stricken children, after Mother died. He had taken her to California so that she could receive the most advanced treatment of the day, with the hope that somehow a miracle would come to pass. But it was not to be. The day he arrived home, we walked solemnly down the station platform to the baggage car, where our mother's casket was unloaded and taken by the mortician. In that moment, we came to know even more about the tenderness of our father's heart.

In the happy home of our childhood, we children knew—and that came of a feeling and not of any declaration—that our parents loved, respected, and honored one another. What a blessing that knowledge has been! When we were children, we felt a certain security because of it. As we grew older, our thoughts and our actions were colored by that remembered example.

My memories of my own wedding day are likewise clear and bright. My wife, Marjorie, and I both stood taller back then; we walked a little faster, and we had far fewer wrinkles. I had only a few dollars in savings, and money was scarce. But we took the plunge anyway. We were in love.

But we were not as much in love then as we are today. We have now been married for more than 60 years. We have grown old together. Through all of these years, we have been blessed in marvelous and remarkable ways. I feel only a sense of gratitude for my wife—for her loyalty, her love, her encouragement, her companionship, her knack for keeping my feet on the ground. I thank the Lord every day for her.

Our children, grandchildren, and great-grandchildren all adore my wife. When our children call home—including our two grown sons, both of whom are accomplished professionally—they never want to talk with me. If I answer the phone, their first words are, "Is Mother there?" They have been saying that for years—and it is wonderful! I am so grateful for this dear woman who has been my companion, my sweetheart, my love, the mother of my children, and the only person in the world who can tell me what to do and I do it—and have been doing it for a very, very long time. As a matter of fact, she doesn't hesitate to tell me. If I go down the wrong track just one step, she pulls me back, and has done so all these many years. I think of how empty life would have been without her. I am sure we have experienced the kinds of problems that most people experience, but somehow we have made it to this station along the road of life. I could not wish for any blessings greater than those I have had in my companionship with my beautiful wife.

God is the designer of the family. He intended that the greatest of happiness, the most satisfying aspects of life, the deepest joys, should come in our associations together and our concerns one for another as fathers and mothers and children, sisters and brothers, aunts and uncles, and so on.

With so much riding on marriage, it stands to reason that the most important decision of life is the decision concerning a companion. Does it seem presumptuous, therefore, to suggest that this is a decision that should be made carefully and prayerfully? If more couples approached this major step by seeking the direction of Heaven, the result would be a greater willingness to work through the challenges that will almost certainly come.

For, unfortunately, all in marriage is not bliss. Jenkins Lloyd Jones said it well:

> There seems to be a superstition among many thousands of our young who hold hands and smooch in the drive-ins that marriage is a cottage surrounded by perpetual hollyhocks to which a perpetually young and handsome husband comes home to a perpetually young and ravishing wife. When the hollyhocks wither and boredom and bills appear, the divorce courts are jammed. . . . Anyone who imagines that bliss is normal is going to waste a lot of time running around

and shouting that he has been robbed. . . . Life is like an old-time rail journey—delays, sidetracks, smoke, dust, cinders, and jolts, interspersed only occasionally by beautiful vistas and thrilling bursts of speed. The trick is to thank the Lord for letting you have the ride.

Indeed, the trick is to enjoy the journey, traveling hand in hand, in sunshine and storm, as companions who love each other.

No one remains young and beautiful, or young and handsome, forever. Stormy weather will hit every household. Connected inevitably with the whole process of marriage is pain—physical, mental, and emotional. Every couple can expect to find challenges along the way. There is much stress and struggle, fear and worry. For many couples, there is the ever haunting battle of economics, for there never seems to be enough money to cover the needs of a family. Sickness strikes periodically. Accidents happen. The hand of death may reach in with dread stealth to take a precious one without warning.

All of this seems to be part of the process of family life. Few indeed are those who get along without experiencing some of it. It has been so from the beginning. Cain quarreled with Abel and then did a terrible thing. How great must have been the grief in the hearts of their parents, Adam and Eve.

Too many who come to marriage have been coddled and spoiled and somehow led to feel that everything must be precisely right at all times, that life is a series of entertainments, that appetites are to be satisfied without regard to principle, that no one could be expected to endure the hardship and challenge that comes at one time or another into most marriages. How tragic are the consequences of such hollow and unreasonable thinking!

Among the most devastating of these tragedies is divorce. It has become a great scourge. In the United States, nearly half of all marriages end in divorce. Behind this startling statistic lies more of betrayal, more of sorrow, more of neglect and poverty and struggle than the human mind can imagine. Millions of those divorced in this nation are lonely, frustrated, insecure, and unhappy. Millions are single parents struggling to rear families alone, carrying burdens beyond their capacity to handle. Millions of children are growing up in single-parent homes from which the parent, usually the mother, is necessarily absent much of the time. These "latchkey children" return from school each day to empty houses where, in many cases, there is inadequate food and only the television set for refuge.

Not only are these children suffering, but all of society is paying a frightful price for their circumstances. As they grow older, the incidence of drug use increases among them. Vast numbers turn to criminal behavior. Inadequately trained, many are unemployed. Some aimlessly squander their lives. Millions have become the flotsam and jetsam of society, washed up on the shore by oceans of neglect, abuse, and frustration, helpless to correct their circumstances. Indeed, of all the problems our society faces, the most serious is the breakdown of the family.

Bitter consequences are seen in the lives of children who do not have a father who loves them, teaches them, protects them, and leads them along the path of life by example and precept. Of those who end up in prison, an alarming percentage come from a broken home where a father abandoned his family and a mother struggled in vain to handle the overpowering odds against her.

I think of a woman I know, an attractive and able young divorcee, the mother of seven children ranging in age from five to sixteen years. One evening, she went across the street to deliver something to a neighbor. As she turned around to walk back home, the echoes of her children's voices as she had walked out of her house a few minutes earlier rang in her ears: "Mom, what are we having for dinner?" "Can you take me to the library?" "I have to get some poster paper tonight." Tired and worn, she looked at her house and saw the light on in each of the rooms. She thought of her children, who were waiting for her to come home and meet their needs. Her burdens felt heavy on her shoulders.

She said: "I remember looking through tears toward the sky and saying, 'Oh, my Father, I just can't do it tonight. I'm too tired. I can't face it. I can't go home and take care of all those children alone. Could I just come to You and stay with You for just one night? I'll come back in the morning.'"

There are so very many like that young mother. Their recognition of a Divine Power is the only thing that keeps them going, because their daily burdens are too much to bear. In loneliness and desperation, they weep and pray.

Why do we have all of these broken homes? What happens to marriages that begin with a couple who are in love and have a desire to be loyal and faithful and true one to another, but that end in heartache and heartbreak?

There is no simple answer. But I fear that marriage, which was once regarded as a sacred sacrament, is increasingly becoming a secular experience. It is too often looked upon as little more than an experiment—if it works, great; if not, try something (or someone) else. People seem to be losing a sense of accountability, not only to one another but to God.

A fundamental issue that accounts for a high percentage of marital problems is selfishness. I say this out of experience—more experience than I would have cared to have—in dealing with such tragedies. I find selfishness to be a major factor in divorce.

Selfishness so often is the basis of money problems, which are a very serious and real factor affecting the stability of family life. Selfishness is at the root of adultery, the breaking of solemn and sacred covenants to satisfy lust. Selfishness is the antithesis of love. It is a cankering expression of greed. It destroys self-discipline. It obliterates loyalty. It tears up sacred covenants. It afflicts both men and women. Selfishness is the great destroyer of happy family life.

There is now and again a legitimate cause for divorce. I am not one to say that it is never justified. But I say without hesitation that this plague among us, which seems to be growing everywhere, is not of God, but rather is the work of the adversary of righteousness and peace and truth.

There is a remedy for all of this. The Lord proclaimed, "What therefore God hath joined together, let not man put asunder" (Matthew 19:6). The remedy for most marital stress is not in divorce. It is in repentance and forgiveness, in sincere expressions of charity and service. It is not in separation. It is in simple integrity that leads a man and woman to square up their shoulders and meet their obligations. It is found in the Golden Rule, a time-honored principle that should first and foremost find expression in marriage.

For marriage to be mutually satisfying, there must be recognition on the part of both husband and wife of the solemnity and sanctity of their union and of the God-given design behind it. Husbands and wives, look upon each other as precious companions, and live worthy of that association. Parents, see in your children sons and daughters of the Almighty, Who will hold you accountable for them. Stand together as their guardians, their protectors, their guides, their anchors.

A wise man once said that "no success in life can compensate for failure in the home." I believe it and commend that statement to all who are seeking a sense of fulfillment and peace, and who are looking for it outside their marriage and their home. It will prove a futile search, for no other relationship—as challenging and as frustrating as marriage can be from time to time—can provide the same security, peace of mind, and sense of well-being.

It is one thing to talk about the importance and sanctity of marriage, and another thing entirely to create such a marriage, day in and day out. It is as C. S. Lewis said:

> [God] allows . . . disappointment to occur on the threshold of every human endeavor. It occurs when the boy who has been enchanted in the nursery by Stories from the Odyssey buckles down to really learning Greek. It occurs when lovers have got married and begin the real task of learning to live together. In every department of life it marks the transition from dreaming aspiration to laborious doing.

Marriage is a contract, a compact, a union between a man and a woman under the plan of the Almighty. It can be fragile.

It requires nurture and time and very much effort. With that in mind, I suggest four cornerstones on which to establish and nurture marriages and homes. I do not hesitate to promise that, with these cornerstones, couples' lives will be enriched and be fruitful of great good, and their joy will be everlasting.

The first cornerstone: *Mutual respect and loyalty to one another.*

I have long felt that happiness in marriage involves a willingness to overlook weaknesses and mistakes. I like what one man said: "Love is not blind—it sees more, not less, but because it sees more, it is willing to see less." Marriage is beautiful when beauty is looked for and cultivated. It can be ugly and uncomfortable when one looks for faults and is thus blinded to virtues. If husbands and wives would only give greater emphasis to the virtues that are to be found in one another and less to the faults, there would be fewer broken hearts and promises, fewer tears, fewer divorces, and much more happiness in their homes.

Each of us is an individual. Each of us is different. There must be respect for those differences, and although it is important and necessary that both the husband and the wife work to ameliorate those differences, there must be some recognition that they exist and that they are not necessarily undesirable. In fact, the differences may make the companionship more interesting.

Unfortunately, some women want to remake their husbands after their own design. Some husbands regard it as their prerogative to compel their wives to fit their standards of what they think to be the ideal. It does not work. It only leads to contention, misunderstanding, and sorrow. There must be respect for each other's interests, there must be opportunities and encouragement for the development and expression of individual talent. Any man who denies his wife the time and the encouragement to develop her talents denies himself and his children a blessing that could grace their home and bless their posterity.

In the Gospel of Matthew we find this classic statement: "For this cause shall a man leave father and mother, and shall cleave to his wife: and they twain shall be one . . . Wherefore they are no more twain, but one" (Matthew 19:4–6). God ordained that marriage partners should be companions. That implies equality.

There is no place in the Judeo-Christian ethic for inferiority or superiority between husband and wife. Does God love and value His daughters less than His sons? Such a notion is unthinkable and totally outside the realm of the character of the Almighty. After the Lord created the earth, and everything upon it, He created man. And then, as the crowning act of creation, He created woman. She was the ultimate of all His creations. It is unwise, unfair, and unenlightened for any man to feel an edge of superiority toward his wife, his daughters, or any woman. No man can demean or belittle his wife without giving offense to her Father in Heaven.

Tragic accounts of troubled marriages all around us speak of dictatorial attitudes among husbands who are bullies in their own homes. A letter once came to my desk from a woman who wrote at length of her troubles. In a spirit of desperation, she asked: "Does a woman have any promise of someday being a first-class member of the human race? Will she always be a piece of chattel wrapped in a chuddar acting only by the permission of the man who stands at her head?"

There is bitter tragedy in the lines of that letter. I fear there are many women who feel that way. Behind this woman's words is a wife who is discouraged, starved for appreciation, ready to give up, and uncertain which way to turn. I picture a husband who has defaulted on his sacred obligations. Calloused in his feelings and warped in his perceptions, he is denying, through his manner of living, the essence of Christian marriage. I do not doubt that there has been fault on her part as well as his, but I am inclined to think that his is the more serious.

A husband who domineers, who belittles and humiliates his wife, and who makes officious demands on her not only injures her but demeans himself and, in all too many cases, plants a similar pattern of future behavior in his sons. Men who are guilty of using their work or civic assignments as excuses to ignore their families, men who are prone to dictate and exercise authority, men who are selfish and brutal in their actions in the home need to forsake their selfish behaviors and change their lives.

It is interesting to me that two of the Ten Commandments have embedded within them the principles of mutual respect and loyalty: "Thou shalt not commit adultery" and "Thou shalt not covet" (Exodus 20:14, 17). Altogether too many men, leaving their wives at home in the morning and going to work, where they find attractively dressed and attractively made-up young women, regard themselves as young and handsome, an irresistible catch. They complain that their wives do not look the same as they did twenty years ago when they married them. To which I reply: Who would, after living with them for twenty years?

The tragedy is that some men are ensnared by their own foolishness. They throw to the wind the most sacred and solemn of covenants they will ever make. They set aside their wives who have been faithful, who have loved and cared for them, who have struggled with them in times of poverty only to be discarded in times of affluence. They leave their children fatherless, often employing every kind of artifice to avoid payment of court-mandated alimony and child support.

Married partners must resist any inclination to cultivate anything more than a cordial, friendly, arm's-length relationship with anyone other than their spouse. More and more, there are invitations to go to lunch, ostensibly to talk about business, and assignments that require men and women colleagues to travel together. Perhaps some of these arrangements are inevitable, but compromising situations can be avoided.

If married partners' first concern and priority is the comfort, the well-being, and the happiness of their spouse, and if they will sublimate personal concerns to that loftier goal, not only will the marriage survive, but their commitment one to another will deepen and their desire to build a lasting relationship will increase. The accumulated wisdom of centuries declares with clarity and certainty that the greater happiness, the greater security, the greater peace of mind, the deeper reservoirs of love are experienced only by those who walk according to time-tested standards of virtue. Only within the marriage relationship can genuine love—love based on serving each other, working together, facing difficulties as partners, walking hand in hand through the ups and downs of daily life—grow and flourish.

I issue a plea for husbands and wives to respect one another and live worthy of the respect of one another, and to cultivate the kind of respect that expresses itself in kindness, forbearance, patience, forgiveness, and true affection, without officiousness or show of authority.

The second cornerstone: *The soft answer.*

The writer of Proverbs long ago declared, "A soft answer turneth away wrath: but grievous words stir up anger" (Proverbs 15:1).

I hear so many complaints from men and women that they cannot communicate with one another. Communication is largely a matter of conversation. They must have communicated when they were courting one another. Can they not continue to speak together after marriage? Can they not discuss with one another, in an open and frank and candid and happy way, their interests, their problems, their challenges, their disappointments, their desires? It seems to me that communication is largely a matter of their talking with one another. It is impossible for them to love someone with whom they don't or won't talk. It is impossible for them to love someone with whom they don't spend time.

But let the talk be quiet, for quiet talk is the language of love. It is the language of peace. It is the language of God. Who can calculate the depth and pain of the wounds inflicted by harsh and mean words spoken in anger? How pitiful a sight are individuals who are strong in many ways but who lose all control of themselves when some little thing, usually of no significant consequence, disturbs their equanimity. In every marriage, there are occasional differences. But I find no justification for tempers that explode at the slightest provocation. "Wrath is cruel, and anger is outrageous" (Proverbs 27:4).

A violent temper is a terrible, corrosive thing. And the tragedy is that it accomplishes no good; it only feeds evil with resentment and rebellion and pain. To all people who have trouble controlling their temper, may I suggest that they seek help to overcome their weaknesses and marshal within themselves the power to discipline their speech.

Spouses who are constantly complaining, who see only the dark side of life, who feel that they are unloved and unwanted, need to look into their own hearts and minds. If there is something wrong, they should try to turn about and put on a smile. To make themselves attractive, they might brighten their outlook. They deny themselves happiness and they court misery if they constantly complain and do nothing to rectify their own faults.

For husbands and wives who may have offended one another, it is time to ask forgiveness and resolve to cultivate respect and affection one for another. It is time to put into practice the principle of the soft answer.

When we raise our voices, tiny molehills of difference become mountains of conflict. There is something significant in the description of Elijah's contest with the priests of Baal: "A great and strong wind rent the mountains, and break in pieces the rocks." That is a vivid description of the arguments that take place between some husbands and wives. But the writer of the scripture continues, "The Lord was not in the wind: and after the wind an earthquake; but the Lord was not in the earthquake: and after the earthquake a fire; but the Lord was not in the fire: and after the fire a still small voice" (1 Kings 19:11–12).

The Voice of Heaven is a still small voice. The voice of peace in the home is a quiet voice. There is need for much discipline in marriage, not of one's companion, but of oneself. "He [or she] that is slow to anger is better than the mighty," as the writer of Proverbs declared (Proverbs 16:32). When couples cultivate the art of the soft answer, it blesses their home, their life together, and their companionship.

The third cornerstone: *Financial honesty.*

I believe that money is the root of more trouble in marriage than all other causes combined. We live in an age of persuasive advertising and skillful salesmanship, all designed to entice us to spend. An extravagant husband or wife can jeopardize any marriage. From personal experience, I believe it to be a good principle for each spouse to have some freedom and independence with everyday, necessary expenditures, while at the same time always discussing and consulting and agreeing on large expenditures. There would be fewer rash decisions, fewer unwise investments, fewer consequent losses, fewer bankruptcies, if husbands and wives would counsel together on such matters and seek counsel from others.

I am confident that there is no better discipline, nor one more fruitful with blessings in the handling of our resources, than obedience to the commandment given to ancient Israel through the prophet Malachi: "Bring ye all the tithes into the storehouse, ... and prove me now herewith, saith the Lord of hosts, if I will not open you the windows of heaven, and pour you out a blessing, that there shall not be room enough to receive it" (Malachi 3:10).

Those who live honestly with God are more likely to live honestly with one another and with their associates. A couple who devote some of their income, even a small percentage, to the good of others will cultivate a discipline in the handling of their resources.

If they live honestly with one another as companions, deal honestly with others, make timely payment of obligations a cardinal principle of their lives, and consult with one another and make decisions in unison, they will be blessed as they do so.

The fourth cornerstone: *Prayer.*

I know of no other practice that will have so salutary an effect on our lives as will the practice of kneeling together as a couple in prayer. The storms that seem to afflict every marriage become of small consequence when we are kneeling before the Lord and addressing Him as suppliant sons and daughters.

Our daily conversations with Him will bless our lives with a joy, strength, and resiliency that can come from no other source. Companionship will sweeten through the years as love strengthens. Appreciation one for another will increase. Children and, later, grandchildren will be blessed with a sense of security that comes of being part of a family wherein dwells the spirit of God as manifest through love, cooperation, and well-being.

Those fortunate enough to have marriages built on these cornerstones will, as the years pass by, be able to say with Elizabeth Barrett Browning:

> How do I love thee? Let me count the ways . . .
> I love thee to the level of everyday's
> Most quiet need, by sun and candle-light.
> I love thee freely, as men strive for Right;
> I love thee purely, as they turn from Praise . . . .
> I love thee with the breath,
> Smiles, tears, of all my life!—and if God choose,
> I shall but love thee better after death.

We Can Save Our
Nation by Saving Our Homes

Society's problems arise, almost without exception, out of the homes of the people. If there is to be a reformation, if there is to be a change, if there is to be a return to old and sacred values, it must begin in the home.

There is no place, no environment more conducive to the development and enactment of virtue than the family. The health of any society, the happiness of its people, their prosperity and their peace, all find their roots in the teaching of children by fathers and mothers, and in the strength and stability of the family. I know this not only because of what I have observed during my eighty-nine years, but because of what I experienced in my childhood home.

When I was a boy, my parents followed a practice they called "family home evening." On a specified evening of the week, we would join as a family to learn together, play together, and enjoy one another's company. My father was a great storyteller, and he often told us stories from his memory.

Mother would warm up the parlor where her grand piano stood, so that we could sing as a family.

We were miserable performers as children. We could do all kinds of things together while playing, but when one of us tried to sing a solo before the others, it was like asking ice cream to stay hard on the kitchen stove. In the beginning, we would laugh and make cute remarks about one another's performance. But our parents persisted. And because they persisted, we sang together. We laughed together. We studied together. And we played and prayed together.

Out of those simple and informal but regular gatherings in the parlor of our old home came something indescribable and wonderful. Our love for our parents was strengthened. My love for my brother and sisters was enhanced. An appreciation for simple goodness grew in all our hearts.

Admittedly, we didn't openly speak about love for one another very much in those days. But we didn't have to. We felt the security, peace, and quiet strength that come to families who pray together, work together, help one another, and feel connected one with another.

Unfortunately, in many homes, we find something far less than this ideal. I was sobered a few years ago by the "Report of the Carnegie Task Force on Meeting the Needs of Young Children," which painted this dismal picture:

> Our nation's infants and toddlers and their families are in trouble. Compared with most other industrialized countries, the United States has a higher infant mortality rate, a higher proportion of low birth-weight babies, a smaller proportion of babies immunized against childhood diseases,

and a much higher rate of babies born to adolescent mothers. Of the twelve million children under the age of three in the United States today, a staggering number are affected by one or more risk factors that undermine healthy development. One in four lives in poverty. One in four lives in a single-parent family. One in three victims of physical abuse is a baby under the age of one.

Such statistics, found in every city and community across the land, ought to be a matter of the gravest concern to every resident of this nation. I recognize, of course, that there have been illegitimate births, that there have been irresponsible fathers and unprepared mothers, that there has been child abuse in its many and depraved forms throughout human history. But the degree of its prevalence in this land must become a matter of concern for all of us.

It is so plainly evident that both the great good and the terrible evil found in the world today are the sweet and the bitter fruits of the rearing of yesterday's children. As we train a new generation, so will the world be in a few years. If we are worried about the future, then we must look today at the upbringing of children.

The evils of the world will continue to escalate unless there is an underlying acknowledgment, even a strong and fervent conviction, that the family is an instrument of the Almighty. It is His creation. It is also the most fundamental and basic unit of society. And it deserves—no, it *demands*—our combined focus and attention.

We go to great lengths to preserve historical buildings and sites in our cities. We need to apply the same fervor to preserving the most ancient and sacred of institutions—the family!

We cannot effect a turnaround in a day or a month or a year. But with enough effort, we can begin a turnaround within a generation, and accomplish wonders within two generations—a period of time that is not very long in the history of humanity.

I'd like to suggest ten specific things we might do to help bring about such a turnaround.

1. *Accept responsibility for our role as parents and fulfill our obligations to our children.*

Every individual in the world is a child of a mother and a father. Neither can ever escape the consequences of parenthood. Inherent in the act of creation is responsibility for the child who is created. None can with impunity run from that responsibility.

Wrote Paul to Timothy, "But if any provide not for his own, and specially for those of his own house, he hath denied the faith, and is worse than an infidel" (1 Timothy 5:8). I am satisfied that Paul is speaking of more than physical nourishment. It is not enough simply for parents to provide food and shelter for their children's physical well-being. There is an equal responsibility to provide nourishment and direction to the spirit and the mind and the heart.

Parents have not just a responsibility but a sacred duty to rear their children in love and righteousness, to teach them to love and serve one another, to observe the commandments of God, and to be law-abiding citizens where they live.

These virtues must be taught at home. There will be little, if any, help from the public schools, which have largely abdicated the teaching of values. Neither should we depend on government to help in this darkening situation. Barbara Bush spoke wisely when she told the 1990 Wellesley graduating class: "Your success as a family—our success as a society—depends not on what happens at the White House, but on what happens inside your house."

Churches can help. Religion is the great conservator of values and teacher of standards. From the days of Sinai to the present, the voice of God has been an imperative voice concerning right and wrong. But when all is said and done, it is parents who have been admonished by God to bring up their children in an atmosphere of spiritual light and truth.

"Probably the best thing that society can do for its toddlers is to make 'parent' an honorable title again," concluded one study. "No job is more important, yet no job is more often taken for granted. We teach work skills but not life skills. . . . Becoming a parent should be . . . a sign of a lasting relationship, not just a passing infatuation; a source of pride, and not remorse. Only then will our children be safe."

2. *Get married and stay married.*

After two years of intense study, the Council on the Family in America reached this conclusion, reported in the *Wall Street Journal* in 1995: "American society would be better off if more people got married and stayed married." What a remarkable conclusion! Nearly any clear-thinking person could have said that without a long and costly study.

In support of its conclusion, the study stated that "children who don't live with both parents are most likely to grow up poor, have problems in school, and get into trouble with the law." The editorial in the *Journal* concluded: "Marriage may be an imperfect institution, but so far in human history no one has come up with a better way to nurture children in a stable society."

Marriage is much more than a civil contract, much more than an agreement between two people. It is an institution essential to the purposes of God. Children are entitled to be born within the bonds of matrimony, and to be raised by a father and mother who honor their marital vows with complete fidelity.

In 1996, there were 7,874,000 fatherless families with children under age eighteen in the United States. In the same year, 1,260,000 children, or 32 percent of all live births, were born to single mothers. How tragic is the desolate statistic of illegitimate births! A lack of self-discipline and of a sense of responsibility is symptomatic of the troubles that afflict us in growing numbers. We have always had illegitimate births in our society, and we likely always will have them. But we cannot tolerate the current increase in this ugly social phenomenon without paying a terrible price.

It should be the blessing of every child to be born into a home where he or she is welcomed, nurtured, loved, and blessed with parents—a father and a mother—who live with loyalty to one another and to their children. This standard means that we must stand strong against the wiles of the world. The accumulated wisdom of centuries declares with clarity and certainty that the greater happiness, the greater security, the greater peace of mind, the deeper reservoirs of love are experienced only by those who walk according to time-tested standards of virtue before marriage and total fidelity within marriage, and that the greatest sense of security and peace of mind is fostered within the family.

If we could only see a resurgence in this land of a man looking to his wife as his equal, his comfort, and his dearest friend, and a woman walking beside her husband, neither before nor behind him, as a companion, and looking to him as the light and strength of her life, we would begin to strengthen families. Children would feel secure in the embrace and love of happy parents, who would instill in them the moral and ethical standards that would guide them throughout their lives. Such marriages would be honorable and secure, and children would be nurtured and loved and reared in those values that are of the very essence of our civilization.

I submit that there is nothing any of us can do that will have greater long-term benefit—particularly for our children, who are our hope for the future—than to rekindle wherever possible the spirit of a happy home and to once again provide a stable family environment where children can develop under the watchful, loving eye of virtuous parents.

3. *Put the father back at the head of the home.*

More than forty years ago, in 1958, the *Reader's Digest* carried an article written by Judge Liebowitz, of New York City, titled "Put Father Back at the Head of the Family." In his capacity as judge, the author spent his days listening to evidence and handing down sentences. He traveled to Europe and discovered that the conditions among the youth there were often much better than in America. He investigated and thought and pondered, and out of his vast experience he came to the conclusion that the easiest, simplest way to reduce delinquency among the young was to put the father back as head of the family.

Far too many families have been denied the leadership and stabilizing influence of a good and devoted father who stands at the side of an able and caring mother in quietly training, gently disciplining, and prayerfully helping the children for whom they are both responsible.

I do not believe that women resent the strong leadership of a man in the home. He becomes the provider, the defender, the counselor, the friend who will listen and give support when needed. Who better than an exemplary father to effectively teach children the value of education, the dead-end nature of street gangs, and the miracle of self-esteem that can change their lives for good?

But how do we get him to claim his place as head of the family? It may be a slow process, but it is worth the effort. We can begin with young boys and teach them, motivate them, and point them in this direction. We will not save them all. But we can save many more than we are now saving.

Several years ago, the *Wall Street Journal* carried an account of a lawyer in Ohio. He spoke of his boyhood, and told how his father took the family for a ride in their old car on a Sunday afternoon. While they were going down the street, a fancy red Cadillac passed them.

The boy asked his father why some people had Cadillacs while their car was an old jalopy. His father responded that everyone couldn't have the same, but that he, his son, had something of tremendous worth that many others did not have, and it was of greater value than any Cadillac. He was a descendant of his father's and mother's families, and there flowed in his veins the best blood of each. This wise father taught his son that although all could not achieve temporal equality, everyone could cultivate that wonderful quality of self-esteem. The boy grew to manhood, studied law, and became a successful professional.

I plead with fathers to resume their role as the head of their homes. Fathers have the basic and inescapable responsibility to stand as head of the family. That does not carry with it any implication of dictatorship or unrighteous dominion. It confers the mandate to provide for the needs of their families. Those needs are more than food, clothing, and shelter. Those needs include righteous direction and the teaching, by example as well as precept, of basic principles of honesty, integrity, service, respect for the rights of others, and an understanding that we are accountable, not only to one another but also to God, for that which we do in this life. One writer observed, "It is not impossible that the true revolutionaries of the twenty-first century will be the fathers of decent and civilized children."

4. *Recognize and value the supreme importance of mothers.*

The home produces the nursery stock of new generations, and parents are the gardeners. In that light, I must emphasize the importance, the value, the singular impact that women have within the fabric of our society and in the makeup of our homes. Mothers have no more compelling responsibility, nor any laden with greater rewards, than the nurture given their children in an environment of security, peace, companionship, love, and motivation to grow and do well.

Mothers provide inspiration and balance; they constitute a reservoir of faith and good works. They are an anchor of devotion and loyalty and accomplishment. As the keepers of the home, they give encouragement to their husbands and they teach and nurture their children. My life has been influenced in a profound and penetrating way by good, talented, faithful, devoted women. Though my mother died when I was twenty, her influence and even the feeling of her presence have stayed with me to the present day. I can say with complete honesty that the only time I have ever allowed myself to think about the assignments and accomplishments that have come my way is when I have pictured my mother and hoped that somehow my life has reflected well on her and her teachings.

This world needs the touch of women and their love, their comfort, and their strength. Our harsh environment needs their encouraging voices, the beauty that seems to fall within their natures, the spirit of charity that is their inheritance. The God in whom so many of us believe has endowed His daughters with a unique and wonderful capacity to reach out to those in distress, to bring comfort and succor, to bind up wounds and heal aching hearts.

If anyone can change the dismal situation into which we are sliding, it is the good women of this country—and, indeed, the world—if they will rise to the challenge and stand above the sleaze and the filth and the temptation that are all around us.

Wives and mothers are the anchors of the family. They bear the children. What an enormous and sacred responsibility that is! They must guard the children because the forces of evil are everywhere. Parents will be fortunate indeed if, as they grow old and look at those whom they brought into the world, they find in them uprightness of life, virtue in living, and integrity in behavior.

The nurture and upbringing of children is more than a part-time responsibility. It is a fact of life that some mothers must work, but far too many do so only to get the means for a little more luxury and a few fancier toys—all at the sacrifice of their children. Mothers who must work have an increased load to bear. Nevertheless, they cannot afford to neglect their children. Children need a mother's supervision in studying, in working inside and outside the home, in the nurturing that only she can adequately give—the love, the blessing, the encouragement, and the closeness of a mother.

Only as I have grown older have I come to realize the great wealth of the home in which I was nurtured, a wealth measured not in dollars but in qualities more precious than dollars. My mother was an educator, a teacher of English. When we children came along, Mother left her profession and remained at home. She gave us a sense of security, an anchor of love that we felt and appreciated.

Although the contributions of women in all walks of life are respected, I hope we will never look down on a homemaker. I appreciate the perspective of author Marie K. Hafen:

> I am distressed that the modern world's devaluation of motherhood is signaling to my daughter and her friends that preparing to be a homemaker, mother, and wife is "no big deal." . . . In truth, learning to be a superb mother is a very big deal. . . . Such a task involves creating and maintaining a total environment of human warmth, intellectual stimulation, and spiritual strength by someone who sees the wellsprings of personal meaning that lie beyond a first glance at a diaper, a frying pan, and a worn tennis shoe.

Women who make a house a home make a far greater contribution to society than those who command large armies or stand at the head of impressive corporations. Who can put a price tag on the influence a mother has on her children, a grandmother on her posterity, or aunts and sisters on their extended family?

We cannot begin to measure or calculate the influence of women who, in their own ways, build stable family life and nurture for everlasting good the generations of the future. The decisions made by the women of this generation will be eternal in their consequences. May I suggest that the mothers of today have no greater opportunity and no more serious challenge than to do all they can to strengthen the homes of America.

5. *Celebrate and treat children as our most priceless treasures.*

The story is told that in ancient Rome a group of women were, with vanity, showing their jewels to one another. Among them was Cornelia, the mother of two boys. One of the women said to her, "And where are your jewels?" Cornelia responded, pointing to her sons, "These are my jewels." Under her tutelage, and walking after the virtues of her life, they grew to become Gaius and Tiberius Gracchus—the Gracchi, as they were called—two of the most persuasive and effective reformers in Roman history. For as long as they are remembered and spoken of, the mother who reared them after the manner of her own life will be remembered and spoken of with praise also.

Our lives have become intensely fast-paced, filled with busyness and a frantic flitting about that was uncharacteristic of earlier ages. Everything from increased mobility to a plethora of time-saving devices has enticed us to pack our lives with so many activities and pursuits that too many of us have lost sight of something that it is of critical importance to families—time together. If our children are really our greatest treasures, it stands to reason that they deserve our greatest attention.

Family members need time with each other. There is no verdict declaring quality time superior to a quantity of time. A proven theory of the behavioral sciences is both simple and profound: Increased interaction leads to increased sentiment. The more time we spend together, the greater the potential for deepening bonds of love, loyalty, trust, and devotion.

Children are of far greater value than any kind of material wealth. Yet, more than thirty years ago, Gertrude Hoffman of the U.S. Children's Bureau reported that nearly a million children in the United States were being left at home daily without adequate supervision while both parents were at work. She went on to say: "There is no way of measuring the emotional damage suffered by inadequately supervised children or the later cost of delinquency which results from this failure."

We are exacting a terrible price in the weakening of the family that occurs when both parents absent themselves from the home each working day while latchkey children wait for their return. When parents do get home, too often they are tired and under such stress and frustration that they cannot give their children the attention and affection they crave and need. We are now seeing the fruits of such hands-off parenting.

Jenkins Lloyd Jones penned sentiments that bespeak common sense:

> The kid who isn't loved knows it. There is no trauma so excruciating as parental rejection. No other form of human cussedness can more efficiently wreck a human life. Yet there persists the superstition that "advantages" are a substitute for affection. They aren't. The finest of the advantages a family can offer can't be found in a department

store, a car dealer's showroom, or a prep school. The only priceless one is the sense of belonging. Otherwise the family becomes a combination café and dormitory. There's no glue in it.

The Carnegie Task Force report referred to earlier concluded: "Children are our most valuable natural resource, but children do not come without families. It is time to develop strategies to conserve and nurture the family environment of our future generations."

6. *Discipline and train children with love.*

When I was a boy, our family lived in the city during the school season and on a small fruit farm during the summer. On that farm we had a large orchard with a variety of fruit trees. When we were in our early teens, my brother and I were taught the art of pruning. Each holiday and Saturday in February and March, while snow was still on the ground, we would go out to the farm where, with our father, we pruned the trees. We learned that you could, in large measure, determine the kind of fruit you would pick in September by the quality of the pruning in February. The idea was to prune in such a way that the developing fruit would be exposed to air and sunlight, uncrowded as it occupied its place on the branch of the tree.

The same principle applies to children. An old and true proverb states, "As the twig is bent, so the tree is inclined." The primary place for building a value system is the home. I read not long ago about a father who pleaded with a judge to lock up his son because he could not control him. I do not doubt that he had tried; but it was too late. Attitudes had been fixed. Habits had become rigid. Our efforts must begin with children when they are young and pliable, when they will listen and learn.

Not long after my wife, Marjorie, and I were married, we built our first home. We had very little money. I did much of the work myself—labor that would be referred to as "sweat equity" today. The landscaping was entirely my responsibility. The first of many trees we planted was a thornless honey locust. It was only a wisp of a tree, perhaps three-quarters of an inch in diameter. It was so supple that I could bend it with ease in any direction. Envisioning the day when its shade would assist in cooling the house in the summer, I put it in a place at the corner of the house where the wind from the canyon to the east blew the hardest. I dug a hole, put in the bare root, packed the soil around it, soaked it with water, and largely forgot it for a long period.

Then one winter day, when the tree was barren of leaves, I chanced to look out the window and was chagrined to see it leaning awkwardly to the west, misshapen and out of balance. I could scarcely believe it. I went out and braced myself against it as if to push it upright. But the trunk was now nearly a foot in diameter. My strength was as nothing against it. I took from my toolshed a block and tackle, attached one end to the tree and another to a well-set post, and then pulled the rope. The pulleys moved a little, and the trunk of the tree trembled slightly. But that was all. It seemed to say, "You can't straighten me. It's too late. I've grown this way because of your neglect, and I will not bend."

In desperation, I finally resorted to drastic measures. I sawed off the great heavy branch on the west side. The saw left an ugly scar more than eight inches across. I stepped back and surveyed my handiwork. I had cut off the major part of the tree, leaving only one branch growing skyward.

More than half a century has passed since I planted that tree. My daughter and her family now live in that home. The other day, I looked again at the tree. It is large. Its shape is better. It is a great asset to the home. But how serious was the trauma of its youth, and how brutal the treatment I used to straighten it.

When the tree was first planted, a piece of string would have held it straight against the forces of the wind. I should have and could have supplied that string with ever so little effort. But I did not, and it bent to the forces that came against it.

I have seen a similar thing occur in the lives of many children. The parents who brought them into the world seem almost to have abdicated their responsibility. The results have been tragic. A few simple anchors would have given them the strength to withstand the forces that shaped their lives. But left alone for too long, they bend to the force of the elements. And the day comes when it appears to be too late.

Children *are* like trees. When they are young, their lives can be shaped and directed, usually without much difficulty. Said the writer of Proverbs: "Train up a child in the way he should go: and when he is old, he will not depart from it" (Proverbs 22:6).

There are parents who, notwithstanding an outpouring of love and a diligent and faithful effort to teach them, see their children grow in a contrary manner and weep while their wayward sons and daughters willfully pursue courses of tragic consequences. For these parents I have great sympathy, and to them I am wont to quote the words of Ezekiel: "The son shall not bear the iniquity of the father, neither shall the father bear the iniquity of the son" (Ezekiel 18:20).

But this is the exception rather than the rule. Nor does the exception excuse others of us from making every effort in showing forth love, example, and correct precept in the rearing of those for whom God has given us sacred responsibility.

I know a wonderful couple whose older children grew up, married at a traditional age, and went forward with their lives in a way that delighted the parents. They became accomplished, responsible, contributing members of society. And then there was a younger boy, a bright and able son. His high school friends pulled him in a different direction, and in time he adopted a lifestyle foreign to the family. He became unkempt. He seemed unable to focus on anything but himself. He did a number of things that brought distress and embarrassment to his parents. His father was distraught. He scolded and threatened, but that only drove his son away from home. His mother wept and prayed. But she controlled her feelings and kept her voice low. She repeatedly expressed to her son her love for him. Though he had left home, she kept his room tidy, his bed made, and the food he liked in the refrigerator. She told him that whenever he felt like coming home, he was welcome.

Months passed while hearts ached. But then the son began coming back occasionally to sleep. Without ever scolding, his mother joked with him, placed delicious meals before him, put her arms around him, and expressed her love openly and frequently. Finally, he began to improve his appearance. He stayed home more. He came to realize that there was no other place as comfortable, no place as secure or happy as the home he had left. He abandoned some of his bad habits. The last time I saw him, he and his mother sang a duet at a public gathering while those who knew their history quietly shed tears of joy at the reconciliation.

Our children are never lost until we give up on them! Love, more than any other thing, will bring them back into the family fold. Punishment is not likely to do it. Reprimands without love will not accomplish it. Patience, expressions of appreciation, and that strange and remarkable power that comes with love and prayer will eventually win through.

I contrast this with another acquaintance of mine, a childhood friend who lived in the same neighborhood. We had a close-knit group of friends growing up, and we all loved each other and loved to go in and out of each other's homes—except, that is, for one home. I confess that I detested the father in that home. His young boys were our friends, but he was my enemy. Why such strong antipathy? Because he whipped his children with strap or stick or whatever was handy when his vicious anger flared at what seemed to be the slightest provocation.

Perhaps I disliked the man so much because of the sharp contrast with the home in which I lived, where we had a father who, by some quiet magic, was able to discipline his family without the use of harsh punishment, though on occasion we may have deserved it.

I have seen the fruits of that neighbor's temper perpetuated in the troubled lives of his children. I have discovered that he was one of that very substantial body of parents who seem incapable of anything but harshness toward their children. I have also come to realize that this man who walks in the memories of my childhood is but one example of uncounted thousands in the world who abuse children in some fashion. The whole tragic picture is one of beatings, kicking, slamming, and, regrettably, in some circumstances, even sexual assault on small children.

I have no disposition to dwell on this ugly picture. I wish only to say that although there is a need for discipline within families, there is never justification for discipline with severity, with cruelty, with bitterness, with anger. It cures nothing and only aggravates the problem.

The primary training, the most effective training, the most persuasive and permanent training of children finds its roots in the home. If the home inflicts harshness, abuse, uncontrolled anger, dishonesty, immorality, and disloyalty, the fruits will be certain and discernible and, in all likelihood, repeated in the generation that follows. If, on the other hand, there is forbearance, forgiveness, respect, consideration, kindness, mercy, and compassion, the fruits again will be discernible and they will be rewarding. The example of wise, fair, honest, and loving parents will do more than anything else in impressing on the minds of children the important principles they need to adopt in their own lives.

7. *Teach values to children.*

Would not all of society benefit if parents could be counted on to teach time-honored principles and values that rear virtuous individuals and lead to a strong society? What then should we teach?

Teach children civility toward others. In recent years, we have witnessed a situation beyond understanding as Yugoslavia has been dismembered into hateful groups killing one another. There seems to be no sense of mercy. The innocent are gunned down without consideration. The hatred seems only to intensify among the Croats, Muslims, Serbs, and Albanians.

Why all this upheaval? We are told that it comes of the fact that for generations in the homes of that land, hatred has been taught—hatred for those of ethnic roots other than one's own. The tragedy of Bosnia-Herzegovina is the bitter fruit of seeds of hatred sown in the hearts of children by their parents. We can protect America against conflict between ethnic groups or religious or diverse groups of any kind. Let it be taught in the homes of our people that we are all children of God, and that as surely as there is fatherhood, there can and must be brotherhood. Conflict among the races will fade when all of us recognize that we are all part of one great family, valued equally by the Almighty—particularly when we treat each other accordingly.

Is this old-fashioned? Of course it is. It is as old as truth itself. Quarreling families are only an expression of the sophistry of the devil.

Teach children tolerance. No one need surrender his or her own beliefs while extending tolerance to those with other beliefs.

Teach them respect—respect for others, respect for the property of others, respect for the opinions of others, respect on the part of men for women and women for men.

Teach them loyalty—loyalty to family, loyalty to friends and associates, loyalty to the institutions of which they are a part, to the nation of which they are citizens, to the flag that flies above them.

Teach them the beauty of freedoms—the marvelous freedoms established by the Bill of Rights, the first ten amendments to the Constitution of this nation.

Teach them obedience to law—where there are disagreements, there are proper and peaceful ways of adjudicating differences.

Teach them the importance of health, of respect for their bodies and minds—they cannot put into them destructive substances without paying a frightful and debilitating price.

Teach them the quality of charity and the meaning of service.

Teach them that there is a Power greater than their own to Whom they may appeal with expectation of help.

Teach them the thrill and joy of learning, for the more they learn, the more they are in a position to learn. Seek to establish an environment conducive to study in the home.

A *Wall Street Journal* editorial, reporting on the scholastic superiority and extraordinary accomplishments of ethnic Asians at the University of California at Berkeley, said of these students:

> The most important factor in the rise of this new American elite is the intense and devoted family relationships that typify the Asian home. . . . They include respect for elders and high standards for children, including hard work at school and off-hours responsibilities that many times still include chores at a relative's business.

Let parents teach their children the sanctity of sex—that the gift of creating life is sacred, that the impulses that burn within us can be and must be disciplined and restrained if there is to be happiness and peace and goodness and a sense of self-worth. Teach them fidelity one to another—that marriage is sacred, that good family relationships are the foundation of good and productive lives. Let there be instilled in the mind of every young man a great salient fact—that every young woman is a daughter of God, and that in offending her, he not only demonstrates his own weakness but also offends his God. Let him understand that to sire a child brings a responsibility that will last as long as he lives.

It is the responsibility of parents to rear children in light and truth. Let the truth be taught by example and precept—that to steal is evil, that to cheat is wrong, that to lie is a reproach to anyone who indulges in it. Teach them to be honest—that an erosion of personal integrity corrodes the soul and the spirit, that a breach in integrity not only brings distrust from others but leaves us wondering whether we can trust ourselves.

Perhaps most important, teach children the meaning and the importance of love, and do so by loving them and letting them experience the warmth, security, and support that such love entails. A popular bumper sticker asks: "Have you hugged your child today?" How fortunate is the child who feels the affection, the acceptance, the unqualified love of his or her parents. That warmth, that love will bear sweet fruit in the years that follow.

8. *Teach children to work.*

I have no idea how many generations ago someone first said, "An idle mind is the devil's workshop." But it is still true. Children need to learn to work. Ideally, they do this by working with their parents—washing dishes with them, mopping floors, mowing lawns, pruning trees and shrubbery, painting and fixing up and cleaning up and doing a hundred other things whereby they learn that labor is the price of cleanliness, progress, and prosperity. Overindulging children only wreaks havoc. Let them grow up with respect for and understanding of the meaning of labor, of working and contributing to the home and its surroundings, with some way of earning some of their own expense money. Hundreds of thousands of youth in this land are growing up with the idea that the way to get something is to steal it.

A little hard work breeds a greater respect for personal and public property. I still remember an experience during my first year in high school. I was eating lunch with some other boys. I peeled a banana and threw the peeling on the ground just as the principal walked by. He asked me to pick up the banana peeling. I say he "asked," but there was a certain steely firmness in his tone. I got off the bench on which I was sitting and picked up the banana peeling and put it in the trash can. There was other litter around the can. He told me that while I was picking up my own trash, I could pick up the trash of others. I did it. I have never thrown another banana peeling on the ground. It leads me to wonder whether graffiti would soon disappear if all those who sprayed it on had to clean it off.

Included in the work we teach our children, may we show them by example that some of our finest work comes through service to others. Selfishness is a destructive, gnawing, corrosive element in the lives of many people. But the antidote to selfishness is service, a reaching out to those about us—those in the home and those beyond the walls of the home. A child who grows up in a home where there are selfish, grasping parents is more likely to develop those tendencies in his or her own life. On the other hand, children who see their father and mother forgo comforts for themselves as they reach out to those in distress will more likely follow the same pattern when they become adults.

9. *Read to and with children.*

Television is perhaps the greatest medium ever discovered to teach and educate and even to entertain. But the filth, the rot, the violence, and the profanity that spew from television screens into our homes is deplorable. It is a sad commentary on our society. The fact that a television set is on six or seven hours every day in most of the homes of America says something of tremendous importance. A study by the American Psychological Association determined that a typical child who begins, at the age of three years, to watch twenty-seven hours of TV a week, will view 8,000 murders and 100,000 acts of violence by the age of twelve years.

Without question, television and the Internet can be addictive. I feel sorry for those who are addicted to the tube, and I worry about those addicted to surfing the Internet, which, like television, has many worthwhile educational benefits but also comes complete with a host of social ills.

I feel sorry for parents who do not read to their young children; conversely, I feel sorry for children who do not learn the wonders to be found in good books. How stimulating it is to get into the minds of great thinkers as they express themselves in language cultivated and polished, concerning great and important issues! I read once that Thomas Jefferson's upbringing centered on the magnificent phrases of the King

James Bible. What an opportunity not only to walk with great men, even to walk with Jehovah Himself, but also to read and savor the majestic language of the prophets of old as that language was translated into beautiful, powerful English. Children should be encouraged to read the great literature of the ages, as well as what is being said by the great minds of our day.

A friend of mine, a doctor of philosophy in one of our great universities, sent me a book that had great meaning for him. It is titled *And There Was Light,* and it tells the story of Jacques Lusseyran, a boy in Paris who, in an accident, was blinded at the age of eight. When darkness surrounded him, however, there came a new light into his life. He was a teenager when the Germans conquered France and hordes of German soldiers marched into Paris. The Vichy government was formed by traitors to the great traditions of a proud and strong nation. This blind boy, a brilliant student, organized a resistance group. He and his associates ran a clandestine operation, getting information and circulating it with a little newspaper printed on a duplicator. Their effort grew until they were distributing more than 250,000 copies an issue. Then he was betrayed, arrested, and sent to Buchenwald. There, in filth and despair, he lived with similar victims. He could not see, but there was a light within him that rose above the tragedy of his circumstances. He survived as a leader among those in that foul camp. The little publication he started became a great newspaper, the *France-Soir.* I read that book and was lifted and strengthened by the story of that remarkable young man.

I have visited the great Vatican Library in Rome, and it was a most inspirational experience to see those old illuminated texts, hundreds and hundreds of years old, that had been preserved for the blessing of mankind. Similarly, I once studied in the British Museum, the great national library of Britain, with its great tall stacks of hundreds of thousands of books.

There is something almost sacred about a great library because it represents the preservation of the wisdom, the learning, and the pondering of men and women of all the ages, accumulated under one roof. I love books. There is something wonderful about a book. We can pick it up. We can heft it. We can read it. We can set it down. We can think of what we have read. It does something for us. We can share great minds, great actions, and great undertakings in the pages of a book.

Emerson was once asked which, of all the books he had read, had most affected his life. His response was that he could no more remember the books he had read than he could remember the meals he had eaten, but they had made him. All of us are the products of the elements to which we are exposed.

Parents know that their children will read. They will read books and magazines and newspapers. Cultivate within them a taste for the best. While they are very young, read to them the great stories that have become immortal because of the virtues they teach. Let there be a corner somewhere in the house, be it ever so small, where they will see at least a few books of the kind on which great minds have been nourished.

10. *Pray together.*

Parents should teach children to pray while they are young. Is prayer such a difficult thing? Would it be so hard for parents to get on their knees with their little children and address the throne of Deity to express gratitude for blessings and to pray for those in distress, as well as for their own needs?

How mighty a thing is prayer! Of that I can testify. How tragic the loss of any family that fails to take advantage of this precious and simple practice.

I believe that there is no adequate substitute for the practice of kneeling together, morning and evening, as a family in prayer. This, more than fine carpets or the latest in window coverings, will make for better and more beautiful homes.

I know of nothing that will work better to ease family tensions, to subtly bring about the respect for parents that leads to obedience, to invite the spirit of repentance that would largely erase the blight of broken homes, than praying together, confessing weaknesses together before the Lord, and invoking His blessings on the home and those who dwell there.

Can we make our homes more beautiful? Yes, through addressing ourselves, as families, to the Source of all true beauty. Can we strengthen our society and make it a better place in which to live? Yes, by strengthening the virtue of our family life through kneeling together and supplicating the Almighty in the name of His Beloved Son.

I know of no better way to cultivate a desire to do what is right than to humbly ask for forgiveness from Him whose right it is to forgive, and to ask for strength to live above weakness.

I know of no better way to develop a spirit of appreciation in children than for all members of the family to kneel and thank the Almighty for His blessings. Such humble expression will do wonders to build within the hearts of children a recognition of the fact that God is the Source of the precious gifts we have.

The world into which our children are moving is complex and difficult. They will inevitably run into heavy seas of adversity. They will need all the strength and the faith parents can give them while they are yet in the home. And they will also need a greater strength that comes of a Higher Power. They must lift the world, but they will need the help of the Lord to do so. While they are young, pray with them that they may come to know the strength that shall always be available in every hour of need.

Society's problems arise, almost without exception, out of the homes of the people. If there is to be a reformation, if there is to be a change, if there is to be a return to old and sacred values, it must begin in the home, with parents instilling within children the virtues that will make them into strong, contributing members of society.

That home may be ever so simple. It may be in a poor neighborhood, but with a good father and a good mother, it can become a place of wondrous upbringing. Sam Levenson tells of growing up in a crowded New York tenement where the environment was anything but good. Here in this slum, his mother reared her eight precious children. He said, "The moral standard of the home had to be higher than that of the street." His mother would say to them when they acted inappropriately, "You are not on the street; you are in our home. This is not a cellar nor a poolroom. Here we act like human beings."

Good homes are not easily created or maintained. They require discipline, not so much of children as of self. They require respect for others, a respect that grows most naturally when we accept the revealed word of the Lord concerning the purpose of life, the sacred nature of the family unit, and the heritage of each individual family member as a child of God.

With effort, we *can* change the course we are on. We must begin with parents. We must provide, to every man and woman, an understanding of the eternal purposes of life, the obligations of marriage, and the responsibilities of parenthood. Then we must teach our youth of all races, languages, and cultures that there is a better way than the way so many are now going. It will take patience. It will take persuasion. It will take the counsel of wise fathers and mothers. It will take inspiration and a spiritual guidance that reaches beyond our own wisdom.

It is within families that truth is best learned, integrity is cultivated, self-discipline is instilled, and love is nurtured. It is at home that we learn the values and the standards by which we guide our lives. It is at home that we come to determine what we will stand for.

The Loneliness of Moral Leadership

In leadership, in standing for principle, there is loneliness. But men and women of integrity must live with their convictions. Unless they do so, they are miserable.

Some years ago, General Mark W. Clark said this of leadership:

All nations seek it constantly because it is the key to greatness, sometimes to survival . . . the electric and the elusive quality known as leadership. Where does juvenile delinquency begin? In leaderless families. Where do slums fester? In leaderless cities. Which armies falter? Which political parties fail? Poorly led ones. Contrary to the old saying that leaders are born not made, the art of leading can be taught and it can be mastered.

What we desperately need today on all fronts—in our homes and communities, in schoolrooms and boardrooms, and certainly throughout society at large—are leaders, men and women who are willing to stand for something. We need people who are honest; who are willing to stand up for decency, truth, integrity, morality, and law and order; who respond to their consciences even when it is unpopular to do so—perhaps *especially* when it is unpopular to do so.

It is important for leaders to learn to speak out in a way that is persuasive without being heavy-handed or offensive. I love Paul's account before Agrippa of his experience on the way to Damascus. When he had fallen to the ground, the Lord instructed him: "But rise, and stand upon thy feet: for I have appeared unto thee for this purpose, to make thee a minister and a witness . . . to open their eyes and to turn them from darkness to light" (Acts 26:16, 18).

The problem with most of us is that we are afraid to stand up for what we believe, to be witnesses for what is true and right. We want to do the right thing, but we are troubled by fears. So we sit back, and the world drifts about us, and society increasingly adopts attitudes and standards of behavior that most of us do not approve of.

By nature I was a timid boy. When I left to serve as a missionary for my church at the age of twenty-three, my father had just one piece of advice. His counsel has become, perhaps, the greatest help of my life. He quoted to me the words of the Lord to the ruler of the synagogue whose daughter was reported dead: "Be not afraid, only believe" (Mark 5:36). I commend these wonderful words to all who are called upon to stand up for what they believe, and to do so articulately and with confidence.

On February 27, 1860, Abraham Lincoln, the Republican presidential candidate, gave one of the more significant speeches of his political career. Among other things, he attacked the proslavery position of his opponent, Stephen A. Douglas. He concluded his presentation with a strong admonition to his party that they hold fast to the beliefs they had espoused: "Neither let us be slandered from our duty by false accusations against us, nor frightened from it by menaces of destruction to the Government nor of dungeons to ourselves. Let us have faith that right makes might, and in that faith, let us, to the end, dare to do our duty as we understand it." Faith is an irreplaceable virtue for all, particularly those who lead—be it a nation, a company, or a family.

There is great loneliness in leadership. This is so because we have to live with ourselves even if it means abandoning other relationships and pursuits. We have to live with our own consciences. We have to live up to our inner feelings. We have to stand for the values and beliefs that we have embraced, adopted, and woven into our characters.

It was ever thus. The price of leadership is loneliness. The price of adherence to conscience is loneliness. The price of adherence to principle is loneliness. I think it is inescapable. The Savior of the world was a man who walked in loneliness. I do not know of any statement more underlined with the pathos of His loneliness than this one: "The foxes have holes, and the birds of the air have nests; but the Son of Man hath not where to lay his head" (Matthew 8:20).

There is no lonelier picture in history than that of the Savior upon the cross, alone, the Redeemer of mankind, the Savior of the world, the Son of God suffering for the sins of us all.

I go back to these words of Paul: "We are troubled on every side, yet not distressed; we are perplexed, but not in despair;

persecuted, but not forsaken; cast down, but not destroyed" (2 Corinthians 4:9).

It is not easy to be virtuous when all about us there are those who criticize or scorn virtue.

It is not easy to be honest when all about us there are those who are interested only in making a fast buck, and who are willing to compromise almost any standard for personal reputation, power, prestige, notoriety, or profit.

It is not easy to be temperate when society scoffs at sobriety.

It is not easy to be industrious in a recreation-oriented society where all about us there are those who do not believe in the value of work.

In leadership, in standing for principle, there is loneliness. But men and women of integrity must live with their convictions. Unless they do so, they are miserable—dreadfully miserable. And though there may be thorns, though there may be disappointment, though there may be trouble and travail, heartache and heartbreak, and desperate loneliness, there will also be comfort and strength and that "peace of God, which passeth all understanding" (Philippians 4:7).

Never in the history of the world has there been a more profound need for leaders of principle to step forward. Never before, at least not in our generation, have the forces of evil been so blatant, so brazen, so aggressive as they are at the present time. Things we dared not speak about in an earlier era are now constantly projected into our living rooms. All sensitivity is cast aside as reporters and political pundits speak with a disgusting plainness of things that can only stir curiosity and lead to evil.

It is not wise, or even possible, to divorce private behavior from public leadership—though there are those who have gone to great lengths to suggest that this is the only possible view of "enlightened" individuals. They are wrong. They are deceived. By its very nature, true leadership carries with it the burden of being an example. Is it asking too much of *any* public officer, elected by his or her constituents, to stand tall and be a model before the people—not only in the ordinary aspects of leadership but in his or her behavior? If values aren't established and adhered to at the top, behavior down the ranks is seriously jeopardized and undermined. Indeed, in any organization where such is the case—be it a family, a corporation, a society, or a nation—the values being neglected will in time disappear.

We are involved in an intense battle. It is a battle between right and wrong, between truth and error, between the design of the Almighty on the one hand and that of Lucifer on the other. For that reason, we desperately need men and women who, in their individual spheres of influence, will stand for truth in a world of sophistry. I have lived long enough now to know that many political campaigns, for example, are the same. I have heard again and again the sweet talk that leads to victory but seems never to be realized thereafter. We need moral men and women, people who stand on principle, to be involved in the political process. Otherwise, we abdicate power to those whose designs are almost entirely selfish.

Great leaders are willing to speak for virtue, for moral standards in a world where filth, sleaze, pornography, and their whole evil brood are sweeping over us as a flood. They will stand up for integrity in the workplace, at home, and indeed anywhere it is called for. We don't have the luxury of retreating to our private cloisters and pursuing only our special private interests. Strong voices are needed. The weight of our stance may be enough to tip the scales in the direction of truth and right.

Inspired leadership demands loyalty—to our associates, to our heritage, to our good names, most certainly to our families, and to the faith to which we subscribe. How marvelous a quality is loyalty! In this world, almost without exception, we must work together as teams. Would anyone question that those on the football field or the basketball court must work together with loyalty one to another if they are to win? It is so in life with each of us. We work as teams, and there must be loyalty among us.

William Manchester, as a young marine, fought through the terrible battle of Okinawa. He was savagely wounded, but later returned to combat again in the hellish fire of the Shuri Line, where thousands on each side perished. Years later, he returned to Okinawa and walked over its once battle-scarred ridges. Reflecting on those earlier brutish days, he wrote: "Men, I now know, do not fight for flag or country, for the Marine Corps or glory or any other abstraction. They fight for one another. Any man in combat who lacks comrades who will die for him, or for whom he is willing to die, is not a man at all. He is truly damned."

Each of us represents the latest chapter in a long line of generations. Included in those generations are forebears, many of whom made terrible sacrifices for that which we have today. They have left us good names that have been safeguarded through the generations. The names we carry are treasured possessions to be kept unsullied, to be passed to the next generation without stain or embarrassment. We must stand up with loyalty to those who have gone before us.

We cannot be indifferent to the great cause of truth and right. We cannot afford to stand on the sidelines and watch the play between the forces of good and evil. Wrote John the Revelator: "I know thy works, that thou art neither cold nor hot: I would thou wert cold or hot. So then because thou art lukewarm, and neither cold nor hot, I will spew thee out of my mouth" (Revelation 3:15–16).

John's imagery is vivid. It points to our critical duty to stand strong, even to become leaders in speaking up on behalf of those causes that make our civilization shine. Each of us can be a leader within our sphere of influence. The adversary of all truth would put into our hearts a reluctance to make an effort; we must cast that fear aside and be valiant in the cause of truth, fairness, and right.

Men and women who desire to contribute in a meaningful way to our society will find their capacity to do so increased by several simple principles. Peter Drucker at one time studied the managers of America's largest business institutions. After much analysis and study, he arrived at the conclusion that "executive ability seems to have little correlation with intelligence, imagination, or brilliance." Rather, he found that effective leaders do four things: (1) they practice conservation of time; (2) they have an eye fixed on new developments; (3) they build on the strengths of their colleagues; and (4) they starve the problems and feed the opportunities.

tive leader practices conservation of time. Time is really all we have, and every individual has an equal portion of it. The trick is to get more out of whatever time is available to us. Men and women who know how to control their time have won half the battle.

Leaders must keep current. They must read and study. They must look to the future rather than live in the past.

Good leaders build on the strengths of their colleagues. No man or woman can do everything alone. Every executive, every leader, every manager, every parent needs around him or her a body of trusted colleagues. Such synergy leads to success. If all the members of an organization do what they ought to do, they will make each other successful.

The fourth principle, however, is ultimately the most intriguing and yet is the least understood. A wise leader starves the problems and feeds the opportunities. What a great concept this is! It is so easy to do just the opposite, to feed the problems and starve the opportunities. I spend a good part of every day wrestling with challenges. It seems that everyone who comes to my office or sends me a letter has a problem.

Not long ago, at the end of a long and tedious day during which I had been faced with several vexatious dilemmas, I said to myself, "How can you keep this up? Constantly dealing with problems of this kind will eat you up." Then I thought of Peter Drucker's statement and said to myself, "Deal with the problems as wisely as you can. Make your decisions. You may be right; you may be wrong. Hopefully, you will be right because you have prayed earnestly over the matter and you have discussed it with your associates. But once these decisions are made, put them behind you and do not worry about them. Turn around, stand tall, put your head up, and look forward to the marvelous opportunities that you have."

It is virtually impossible for a leader to see the big picture, or to be successful, unless he or she both appreciates the magnificent potential of human beings and insists on aiming for excellence. I first read the words of Hamlet's famous soliloquy nearly seventy years ago, in a college English class: "What a piece of work is man! how noble in reason! how infinite in faculty! in form and moving how express and admirable! in action, how like an angel! in apprehension, how like a god! the beauty of the world! the paragon of animals!"

Admittedly, these words of Hamlet were spoken in irony. And yet there is so much truth in them. They describe the great potential excellence of men and women. If Shakespeare had written nothing else, he would have been remembered for those few words of soliloquy. They go hand in hand with these words of David: "When I consider thy heavens, the work of thy fingers, the moon and the stars, which thou hast ordained; What is man, that thou art mindful of him? And the son of man that thou visitest him? For thou hast made him a little lower than the angels, and hast crowned him with glory and honour" (Psalm 8:3–5).

David's magnificent words declare the wonder of humankind. We are more than a son or daughter of Mr. and Mrs. So-and-So who reside in such-and-such a place. We are a part of the family of God, with a tremendous potential for excellence.

The distance between mediocrity and excellence can be ever so small. As we see during every olympiad, that difference can be measured in hundredths of a second. A little extra effort can result in a tremendous difference.

We would all do well to walk a higher road of excellence. Not long ago, I picked up an old book and reread Lytton Strachey's *Life of Florence Nightingale*. My rereading brought a new sense of admiration and respect for this great young woman of England who made a difference.

She was born to the upper class, born to party and to dance, to go to the races and look pretty in society. But she would have none of it. Even her parents could not understand her. Her overwhelming desire was to alleviate pain and suffering, to hasten healing, to make less dreadful the hospitals of the day. She never married. She devoted herself to nursing and became expert according to the training then available.

Britain became embroiled in the Crimean War. Miss Nightingale had friends at the head of the government, and she relentlessly pursued and persuaded them until she was appointed head of the hospital in Scutari, where thousands of the war victims were brought. The picture that greeted her there was one of absolute despair. An old warehouse served as a hospital. The sanitary conditions were terrible. The cooking facilities were horrid. Wounded men were crowded in great rooms filled with foul odors and the cries of the suffering.

This frail young woman, with those she had recruited to accompany her, set to work. They beat down the walls of bureaucracy. Wrote Mr. Strachey:

For those who watched her at work among the sick, moving day and night from bed to bed, with that unflinching courage, with the indefatigable vigilance, it seems as if the concentrated force of an undivided and unparalleled devotion could hardly suffice for that first portion of her task alone. Wherever, in those vast wards suffering was at its worst and the need for help was greatest, there, as if by magic, was Miss Nightingale.

The beds that held the suffering men stretched over four miles, with barely space between each bed to walk. But somehow, within a period of six months,

> . . . the confusion and the pressure in the wards had come to an end; order reigned in them, and cleanliness; the supplies were bountiful and prompt; important sanitary works had been carried out. One simple comparison of figures was enough to reveal the extraordinary change: the rate of mortality among the cases treated had fallen from 42 percent to 22 per thousand.

This amazing leader had brought to pass an absolute miracle. Lives by the thousands were saved. Suffering was mitigated. Cheer and warmth and light came into the lives of men who otherwise would have died in that dark and dreadful place.

The war ended. Florence Nightingale might have gone back to London a heroine. The public press had sung her praise. Her name was familiar to everyone. But she returned incognito to escape the adulation she might have received.

She continued her work for another fifty years, changing both military and civilian hospitals, until she died at an advanced age. Perhaps no other woman in the history of the world has done so much to reduce human misery as this lady with the lamp. Her life was a life of excellence. Though lonely from time to time, her life was one of moral leadership.

My wife likes to tell the story of a friend of hers who, when she was a little girl, was left an orphan. She scarcely knew her mother. As she grew, she wondered about her mother: What kind of a girl, what kind of a woman was she? One day she came across her mother's old report card. The teacher had noted on that card, "This student is excellent in every way." When she read that, her entire attitude changed. She recognized that her mother had been a woman of excellence. She took on the patina of excellence herself and became a remarkable woman in her own right. She married an accomplished man, and their children have distinguished themselves for their excellence.

I recall a concert I attended in the Salt Lake Tabernacle. The music was provided by the Tabernacle Choir, the Utah Symphony, and the King's Singers. The result was such excellence! The first time I heard the King's Singers I was entranced with their music. They are six Englishmen who sing together everything from the old madrigals to modern pop. They come from different backgrounds, but each is a consummate performer. One can only imagine how many hundreds of hours, lonely hours of individual rehearsal and practice over many years, were required to develop the excellence they now display with seeming ease.

There is nothing in all the world so satisfying as a task or performance well done. There is no reward so pleasing as that which comes with the mastery of a difficult problem or challenge. My plea is that we constantly take the position that every one of us can do better than we are now doing. We are in a constant search for excellence. That search must be continuous and never-ending. It must be consuming and unrelenting. As a nation and as a people, we will not rise to a position of excellence before the world until we have begun to restore and rebuild a foundation of moral, ethical, and spiritual strength. Happily, such a lofty and crucial pursuit does not require genius. But it does require endurance and commitment.

A verse in Ecclesiastes reminds us that "the race is not to the swift, nor the battle to the strong" (Ecclesiastes 9:11). Life's winners are generally those who endure to the end. What tremendous strength there is in commitment! What tremendous strength there is in singleness of purpose, in giving oneself without reservation to the accomplishment of a great and good purpose. What marvelous results follow commitment made to God and His teachings, to the virtues that make us strong morally and physically.

Wrote the poet Emerson:

> So nigh is grandeur to our dust,
> So near is God to man,
> When duty whispers low, *Thou must,*
> The youth replies, *I can.*

When the apostle Paul was a prisoner of Nero in Rome, he wrote: "God hath not given us the spirit of fear; but of power, and of love, and of a sound mind. Be not thou therefore ashamed of the testimony of our Lord" (2 Timothy 1:7–8). To every virtuous, principled person, I commend this stirring injunction. This is the spirit that will transform and reform the world.

Let us take upon ourselves the name of the Lord and then, with faith, go forth to share with relevance that which will affect the lives of all humanity and bring peace and joy to the world. The world needs a generation of men and women of learning, influence, and faith who can and will stand up and, in sincerity and without equivocation, declare that God lives and that Jesus is the Christ.

Without question, we find our greatest example to follow in the Son of God. He is the greatest example of excellence in all the world. He condescended to come to earth under the most humble of circumstances. He grew up as the son of Joseph the carpenter. He struggled with the adversary on the Mount of Temptation. He came forth resplendent and beautiful and magnificent to teach the world. During His brief ministry, He brought more truth, more hope, more mercy, more love than anyone else who has ever walked the earth. He died on Calvary's cross for each of us. He was the great paragon of righteousness, the only perfect man to ever walk the earth. His was the wondrous example toward which we might all point our lives in our eternal quest for excellence.

None of us will become perfect in a day or a month or a year. We will not accomplish it in a lifetime, but we can begin now, starting with our more obvious weaknesses and gradually converting them to strengths as we go forward with our lives. This quest may be a long one; in fact, it will be lifelong. It may be fraught with many mistakes, with falling down and getting back up again. And it will take much effort. But we must not sell ourselves short. We must make a little extra effort. We would be wise to kneel before our God in supplication. He will help us. He will bless us. He will comfort and sustain us. He will help us to do more, and be more, than we can ever accomplish or become on our own.

Tremendous is our opportunity to reach beyond the hoped-for goal of wealth and worldly success to build and strengthen others, to relieve suffering, to aid in making the world a better place, to be as a light. Tremendous also is our potential for leading out and standing up, in every arena of our lives, for the virtues that will make our individual lives, our families, and our society strong and vibrant.

No nation can rise above the strength of its homes or the virtue of its people. The time has come for good people everywhere to demonstrate that they stand for something—something that is virtuous and clean and worthwhile. To that end, may we move forward with faith in the Almighty, and with a determination to live virtuous lives and to return to our society the element of goodness on which it was founded.

Notes

Introduction
The Secularization of America

Page xiii　'Tis fine to see the Old . . .
Henry Van Dyke, "America for Me," in *The Poems of Henry Van Dyke* (New York: Charles Scribner's Sons, 1911), 167–68.

Page xvi　"In the name of God, . . .
"Mayflower Compact, 1620," in *The Harvard Classics, American Historical Documents 1000–1904*, ed. Charles W. Eliot (New York: P. F. Collier and Son, 1910), 43:62; spelling modernized.

Page xvii　"As the British Constitution . . .
"Kin Beyond the Sea," *North American Review*, September 1878.

Page xx　"Because you-know-Who . . .
Wall Street Journal, 31 July 1996, A14.

Page xx　It would be peculiarly . . .
"Washington's First Inaugural Address, 1789," in *The Harvard Classics, American Historical Documents 1000–1904*, ed. Charles W. Eliot (New York: P. F. Collier and Son, 1910), 43:242.

Page xxiii　We try to gamble . . .
Wall Street Journal, 14 August 1998, W11.

One
Love: The Lodestar of Life

Page 4   One of the grand errors . . .
Sydney J. Harris, *Deseret News.*

Page 10   He drew a circle that . . .
Edwin Markham, "Outwitted," in *The Book of Poetry*, selected and annotated by Edwin Markham (New York: William H. Wise and Co., 1927), 265.

Two
Where There Is *Honesty,*
Other Virtues Will Follow

Page 20   "Good name in man and woman, . . .
William Shakespeare, *Othello*, III, iii.

Page 22   The costs of a hijacking . . .
Reprinted from *Christian Science Monitor* in *Deseret News*, 21 April 1978, A3.

Page 23   We will never bring disgrace . . .
Adapted from the ephebic oath, see Phillip Harding, ed. and trans., *Translated Documents of Greece and Rome 2; From the End of the Peloponnesian War to the Battle of Ipsus* (Cambridge: Cambridge University Press, 1985), 133–135.

Page 25   "In war-time, truth is . . .
The Second World War, vol. 5, *Closing the Ring* (Boston: Houghton Mifflin, 1951), 383.

Page 30   "An honest man's the noblest . . .
Alexander Pope, "Essay on Man," Epistle IV, line 248, in *Pope Poetical Works* (Oxford: Oxford University Press, 1966), 275.

Page 31   It was a majestic-looking tree . . .
As quoted in Donald T. Phillips, *Lincoln on Leadership: Executive Strategies for Tough Times* (New York: Warner Books, 1992), 55–56.

Page 32   The heights by great men . . .
Henry Wadsworth Longfellow, "The Ladder of Saint Augustine," stanza 10, as quoted in *Poems That Lift the Soul* (Salt Lake City: Shadow Mountain, 1998), 307.

Page 32   "I have been asked what . . .
As quoted in *BYU Today*, September 1992, 21.

Three
Making a Case for *Morality*

Page 38   According to a 1997 nationwide survey . . .
Wirthlin Worldwide/Family Research Council study, Fall 1997.

Page 40   "Hollywood dream factory"
Michael Medved, *Hollywood vs. America* (New York: Harper Perennial, 1992).

Page 51   "A world in which everyone . . .
Channing Pollock, "The World's Slow Stain," in *Reader's Digest*, June 1960, 77.

Four
Our Fading *Civility*

Page 58   "People might think of a civilized . . .
Royal Bank of Canada Newsletter, vol. 76, no. 3, May–June 1995.

Page 61   Every action in company ought . . .
As quoted in William J. Bennett, *The Spirit of America* (New York: Touchstone, 1997), 152–153.

Page 63   "He jests at scars . . .
William Shakespeare, *Romeo and Juliet*, II, ii, 1.

Page 67   "How prudently most men creep . . .
As quoted in John Wesley Hill, *Abraham Lincoln—Man of God*, 4th ed. (New York: G. P. Putnam's Sons, 1927), 146.

Page 67   Who gives himself with his alms . . .
James Russell Lowell, *The Vision of Sir Launfal* (Chicago: Ainsworth and Co., 1901), part II, stanza 8.

Five
Learning: "With All Thy Getting Get Understanding"

Page 74   Nearly half of the nation's . . .
New York Times, 9 September 1993, A1.

Page 74   What is the mystery . . .
Jim Squires, "Television's Civil War," *Wall Street Journal*, 8 October 1990, A12.

Page 75   We have lived to see . . .
C. S. Lewis, "De Descriptione Temporum," in *Selected Literary*

Essays, ed. Walter Hooper (Cambridge, England: Cambridge University Press, 1969), 4.

Page 76 [T]he great thing is that . . .
Joshua Liebman, "Getting the Most Out of Life," *Reader's Digest,* May 1946, 113.

Page 78 There is no ingenious mind . . .
Discourses of Brigham Young (Salt Lake City: Deseret Book, 1954), 382.

Six
The Twin Virtues of *Forgiveness* and *Mercy*

Page 82 "A piece of string, . . .
Guy de Maupassant, "A Piece of String," in *The Complete Short Stories of Guy de Maupassant* (Garden City, New York: Hanover House, 1955), 152.

Page 83 "We have grasped the mystery . . .
As quoted in Louis Fischer, *The Life of Mahatma Gandhi* (New York: Harper and Row, 1950), 349.

Page 86 "With malice toward none, . . .
"Second Inaugural Address, 4 March 1865," in *Selected Writings and Speeches of Abraham Lincoln,* ed. T. Harry Williams (New York: Hendricks House, Inc., 1943), 261.

Page 89 The quality of mercy is not strained, . . .
William Shakespeare, *The Merchant of Venice,* IV, i, 184–195.

Page 92 Remember!—It is christianity . . .
The Life of Our Lord (London: Associated Newspapers, 1934; reprint, Philadelphia: Westminster Press, 1934), 124–127.

Seven
Thrift and Industry: Getting Our Houses in Order

Page 96   You count me out fifty . . .
Discourses of Brigham Young (Salt Lake City: Deseret Book, 1954), 291.

Page 97   Remember that Time is Money . . .
Benjamin Franklin, as quoted in William J. Bennett, *The Spirit of America* (New York: Touchstone, 1997), 284–285.

Page 100   "Back in the 1950s . . .
Quoted in *Deseret News*, 18 December 1998, C1.

Page 101   Interest never sleeps nor sickens . . .
J. Reuben Clark, Jr., in *One Hundred Eighth Annual Conference of The Church of Jesus Christ of Latter-day Saints*, April 1938, 103.

Eight
Gratitude: A Sign of Maturity

Page 110   "This liberty will look easy . . .
Maxwell Anderson, *Valley Forge, A Play in Three Acts* (New York: Samuel French, Ltd., 1934), 110.

Page 111   Grow old along with me . . .
Robert Browning, "Rabbi Ben Ezra," in *The Poems and Plays of Robert Browning* (New York: The Modern Library, Random House, Inc., 1934), 289.

Nine
Optimism in the Face of Cynicism

Page 119   Do not let us speak . . .
"These Are Great Days," in *Winston S. Churchill: His Complete Speeches*, ed. Robert Rhodes James (New York: Chelsea House Publishers, 1974), 6:6500.

Page 119   We shall not flag or fail . . .
"Wars Are Not Won by Evacuation," in ibid., 6231.

Page 122   Sir Walter Scott was a trouble . . .
Deseret News, 20 October 1960.

Ten
Faith: Our Only Hope

Page 130   Behind him lay the great Azores . . .
Joaquin Miller, "Columbus," in *One Hundred and One Famous Poems*, comp. Roy J. Cook (Chicago: Contemporary Books, Inc., 1958), 58–59.

Page 130   "Thank God. I have done . . .
As quoted in David Howarth, *Trafalgar: The Nelson Touch* (New York: Atheneum, 1969), 150.

Page 132   "If America is to grow . . .
Laurence M. Gould, *This Week Magazine*, 7 August 1966.

Page 132   As we gather . . .
Wall Street Journal, 24 December 1992, A4.

Page 133   What could be more ironic . . .
Salt Lake Tribune, 13 December 1992, A41.

Page 138   At every one of the places . . .
Elizabeth Wood Kane, *Twelve Mormon Homes Visited in Succession on a Journey through Utah to Arizona* (Philadelphia: William Wood, 1874).

Marriage
What God Hath Joined Together

Page 151   There seems to be . . .
Deseret News, 12 June 1973, A4.

Page 156   "No success in life . . .
J. E. McCulloch, *Home: The Savior of Civilization*, 1924, 24.

Page 156   [God] allows . . . disappointment . . .
C. S. Lewis, The Screwtape Letters (New York: Macmillan Publishing Co., 1961), 13.

Page 157   "Love is not blind . . .
The Treasure Chest (New York: Harper Collins, 1965), 168.

Page 158   Will she always be . . .
A chuddar is a large square shawl worn by women in India.

Page 165   How do I love thee . . .
Elizabeth Barrett Browning, "Sonnets from the Portuguese XLIII," in *The Complete Poetical Works of Mrs. Browning*, ed. Harriet Waters Preston (Boston: Houghton Mifflin Co., 1900), 223.

Notes

The Family
We Can Save Our Nation
by Saving Our Homes

Page 168   Our nation's infants and toddlers . . .
"Starting Points: Meeting the Needs of Our Youngest Children: Report of the Carnegie Task Force" (New York: Carnegie Corporation, April 1994).

Page 171   "Your success as a family . . .
As reported in *Deseret News*, 1 June 1990.

Page 171   "Probably the best thing . . .
U.S. News & World Report, 25 April 1994, 10–11.

Page 171   "Marriage may be an imperfect . . .
Wall Street Journal, 25 April 1995, A20.

Page 174   The boy asked his father . . .
Michael L. King, "Fatherhood and the Black Man," *Wall Street Journal*, 6 June 1988.

Page 175   "It is not impossible . . .
John Lukacs, *The Passing of the Modern Age* (New York: Harper and Row, 1972), 82.

Page 177   I am distressed that the . . .
Bruce C. Hafen and Marie K. Hafen, *The Belonging Heart* (Salt Lake City: Deseret Book Co., 1994), 292–293.

Page 179   "There is no way . . .
Deseret News, 13 January 1966, C1.

Page 179   The kid who isn't loved . . .
Deseret News, 13 July 1968.

Page 187   The most important factor . . .
Wall Street Journal, 30 May 1995, A14.

Page 190   Television is perhaps the . . .
See *U.S. News & World Report*, 11 September 1995, 66.

Page 194   "The moral standard . . .
Sam Levenson, *Everything But Money* (New York: Simon and Schuster, 1966), 145.

Epilogue
The Loneliness of Moral Leadership

Page 197   All nations seek it . . .
Quoted in Thomas Jefferson Research Center Bulletin, No. 23, December 1967.

Page 199   "Neither let us be . . .
Quoted in *Lincoln On Leadership*, 149.

Page 202   "Men, I now know . . .
William R. Manchester, *Goodbye Darkness: A Memoir of the Pacific War* (Boston: Little, Brown, 1980), 391.

Page 203   "Executive ability seems . . .
See Peter F. Drucker, *The Effective Executive* (New York: Harper & Row, 1993), as quoted in *Fortune*, February 1967, 140 ff.

Page 205   "What a piece of work . . .
William Shakespeare, *Hamlet*, II, ii, 316–322.

Page 207   The confusion and the pressure . . .
Lytton Strachey, *Life of Florence Nightingale*, Travelers Library (Doubleday, Doran & Co., 1934), 1186.

Page 209   So nigh is grandeur . . .
Ralph Waldo Emerson, "Voluntaries III," in *The Complete Works of Ralph Waldo Emerson: Poems* (Boston: Houghton Mifflin and Co., 1904), 9:207.

Index